MW00850106

THE HIGHLANDS CIRCLE
—— Carnegie Mellon ——

September 2010

Presented to
Judith and Frank J. Marshall

~ Members since 2005 ~

MANHATTAN PROJECT TO THE SANTA FE INSTITUTE

Manhattan Project to the Santa Fe Institute

The Memoirs of George A. Cowan

George A. Cowan

UNIVERSITY OF NEW MEXICO PRESS
ALBUQUERQUE

© 2010 by the University of New Mexico Press
All rights reserved. Published 2010
Printed in the United States of America
14 12 11 10   1 2 3 4

Library of Congress Cataloging-in-Publication Data
Cowan, G. A. (George A.), 1920–
Manhattan Project to the Santa Fe Institute : the memoirs of
  George A. Cowan / George A. Cowan.
      p. cm.
    Includes index.
    ISBN 978-0-8263-4870-8 (cloth : alk. paper)
    1. Cowan, G. A. (George A.), 1920– 2. Chemists—United States—
Biography. 3. Manhattan Project (U.S.)—History.
4. Los Alamos National Laboratory—History. 5. Santa Fe
Institute (Santa Fe, N.M.)—History. 6. Businessmen—
New Mexico—Los Alamos—Biography. 7. Los Alamos (N.M.)—
Biography. 8. Philanthropists—United States—
Biography. I. Title.
    QD22.C69A3 2010
    540.92—dc22
    [B]
                              2009030992

Unless otherwise cited, all photographs are courtesy of the author,
Dr. George A. Cowan, and they are reproduced with his permission
for this book only. No other reproduction of images supplied by
Dr. Cowan is allowed.

Frontispiece: Photograph courtesy Los Alamos National Laboratory

Contents

Introduction

In 1938 German chemists Otto Hahn and Fritz Strassmann found that when a uranium atom captured a neutron and became highly excited, it sometimes split into two lighter elements and simultaneously converted a tiny fraction of its mass to a very large pulse of energy. Soon two of their compatriots, theoretical physicists Lise Meitner and nephew Otto Frisch, found an explanation. They compared the process, which they called fission, to a vibrating soap bubble breaking into two smaller bubbles. Since additional neutrons were emitted in this process, scientists speculated that a sufficient amount of uranium in an appropriate geometry might sustain a rapidly multiplying "chain" reaction. The notion of an atom bomb suddenly moved from science fiction to imminent reality.

I brought the newspaper announcement of the discovery of fission to my college sophomore physics class at Worcester Polytechnic Institute. Dr. Morton Masius devoted his lecture to the article and concluded that an atom bomb was unlikely. It was an event that would eventually draw me deeply into science and shape the rest of my life.

After receiving a bachelor's degree in chemistry in 1941 from Worcester Polytechnic Institute, I became a member of the cyclotron research group at Princeton. In May 1942 the group moved to the University of Chicago to join the newly formed Manhattan Project, the huge government crash program designed to produce one or more atomic bombs. I remained with the Project through its termination in 1946. In my subsequent career in nuclear chemistry and physics at Los Alamos, I was largely involved with weapons test diagnostics and assessment of foreign technology. The problems were challenging and attracted many gifted scientists. We developed much of what is currently termed *nuclear forensics*. I was also provided with time and resources to pursue basic research.

In describing some of the historic events in which I played a supporting role, I hope to nurture the interest of young people in science. I am quite sure that those who choose to become scientists will be deeply challenged by new surprises, some of them comparable to, or exceeding, the discovery of fission. An old friend, Peter Carruthers, said, "Science is a bubble, expanding into an infinite sea of ignorance. As the interface gets bigger, important questions keep multiplying."

My decision to undertake this memoir was also influenced by a rather different topic. I have searched my early history to help explain what I became as an adult. Untangling the complex mixture of innate and external influences that eventually made me a nuclear scientist, the founder of a center for research on complexity science, and a part-time entrepreneur in finance has been a fascinating challenge.

When did I become a scientist? I can't remember any particular event that might qualify as an epiphany. I now believe that I must have begun very early. Some prominent developmental psychologists have asserted that all normal babies are born scientists. Most of what they experience is new. They have to constantly construct hypotheses and test them. However, after a few birthdays, most toddlers become less curious about their environments. They have learned enough "scripts" to cope with daily events. Some, for reasons that may be innate or cultural or both, retain and enlarge their world of wonder. Apparently, I was one of them. In constructing this account, I've found it necessary to delve back in time as far as I can, possibly to age two.

In recent years I have developed an increasing interest in neuroscience and its relationship to behavior and the world of human affairs. In 1991 when, at age seventy-one, I left the presidency of the Santa Fe Institute, I decided to study infant brain development and behavior. Developmental psychology deals with externally observable behavior of infants and toddlers. Neuroscience looks inside the skull and deals with the way the brain works. Clearly, parts of these two fields of study must overlap. A research scientist can stimulate one or more of the senses with a particular signal and observe the related neuronal response. But when an individual is independently selecting among various incoming signals from the environment and attending to some of them, deducing connections between the environment, neuronal activity, and behavior is very difficult. Nevertheless, I felt that additional research might demonstrate how observable patterns of regional ongoing and specifically evoked neuronal activity are related to developing patterns of behavior.

My belief was based in part on the fact that the brain governs behavior from the moment of birth. The brain is the most complex organ we know. An experiment conducted by Dr. Andrew Meltzoff, a developmental psychologist at the University of Washington, serves to illustrate an early aspect of its complexity. The circumstances of a newborn infant's delivery were arranged so that Dr. Meltzoff's face was the very first object seen when the baby opened her eyes. Dr. Meltzoff stuck out his tongue. The baby stuck out her tongue. The visual cortex had registered its very first image, recognized a relationship to self, transferred this information to an innate map of its own body, identified the correct region, and activated the imitative motor response. What a remarkable chain of events in the baby's first moments of life!

At birth the brain contains about one hundred billion neurons. These are the cells that enable us to think and remember. The number of neurons doesn't change much during subsequent development. However, they become increasingly connected to one another by stimulating signals from the external environment. Although many chains are programmed in the womb to enable the newborn infant to deal with its environment, much of the brain's instruction occurs after birth. New chains constantly form as they incorporate memories and patterns of acquired skills. The number of potential arrangements is almost incomprehensibly large, much more than enough to provide a diary of every conscious moment of existence. Marcel Proust wrote an extensive series of novels, much of it autobiographical, in his *Remembrance of Things Past*. He reconstructed daily events in exquisite detail. He was continuing to work on a seemingly endless journal of remembrances when he died. I think of Proust when I find myself unearthing veins of memory that become constantly richer as they are explored.

My memories have helped me identify some apparent relationships between my early environment and the person I became. However, much seems to have been due to chance. If there is a continuing, unbroken thread, it must be related to the innate curiosity that tended to keep me more interested in my vast ignorance than in my acquired fragmentary expertise. It was also essential that I learned habits of critical thinking that prompted me to examine conventional wisdom and beliefs. They profoundly affected my behavior. Fortunately, I found my first professional employment with people who valued and nurtured these habits. I owe them a great debt.

1 My Early Environment

I was born in Worcester, Massachusetts, on February 15, 1920. My parents were Jewish immigrants from Trochenbrod, a village about 150 miles northeast of Lwow in the Ukraine. It was eradicated, together with its people, by occupying Germans in 1942. Jonathan Safran Foer memorialized it as the fictional Trachimbrod in his wonderful, simultaneously hilarious and tragic 2002 novel *Everything Is Illuminated*. I almost certainly would have had a short adulthood if my parents had remained in Trochenbrod.

Two enormously important constitutional amendments were adopted in the United States in the year of my birth. The Eighteenth was the Prohibition Amendment. The Nineteenth was the Women's Suffrage Amendment. Both profoundly affected the culture that contributed to my early development. It is the Eighteenth that I particularly remember. It taught many millions of law-abiding citizens to become part-time chemists, producers of beer and wine. The amendment made it illegal to manufacture or sell alcoholic beverages for external distribution. It was legal so long as they were used at home. An illegal solution was to buy what was needed from bootleggers. Both solutions were popular and widely practiced. My mother made wine from dried cherries. My father had Canadian rye delivered to the house about once a month. Our neighbors made beer.

Prohibition was an effort to change generally accepted behavior by edict. It was a failure. The Eighteenth Amendment was repealed in 1933. After nearly fourteen years of national prohibition, the principal effect on our culture was to nurture a widespread disregard of civil authority. It was an important part of my environment in my formative years.

Memories of my own early childhood begin around age two. My mother loved music, particularly opera. She played arias on a windup Victrola in our living room. I remember sitting on the floor, looking up at the dark mahogany record player, and listening to Feodor Chaliapin singing Moussorgsky's "Song of the Flea" in Russian. I suspect I could hum it before I could talk.

I also sat on the floor when I learned to count with toothpicks that my mother arranged in groups. They had names—one, two, three, and so on. I had semantic problems. Why not one, three, two? I was told this was forbidden. I suspect I was initially offended by the arbitrariness of language, particularly with respect to the names of numbers.

Proust's reference to madeleines in his *Remembrance* somehow makes me smell chocolate cake. Its fragrance was part of the stream of messages that bombarded my senses from the moment of birth. New information had to be sorted out and remembered or forgotten. Novelty was delightful. My brain was faithfully making lists of faces, sounds, tastes, textures, and smells. I'd search for more until I fell asleep. I think now of how curiosity is innate in babies.

The one sense that probably never slept was smell. At first the odors were associated with mother and food, then with soap, and then with other people, pets, flowers, and mysterious stuff that drifted in the window. Years later I realized that my sense of smell was an enormously skillful chemistry laboratory. Each odor was due to a particular molecule or set of molecules. My nose and brain could identify and remember thousands of them and attribute most of them to their source.

I had an older sister, Charlotte (aka Lottie), and a younger brother, Milton. Charlotte must have considered me a remarkable addition to her collection of toy dolls. She paid me a great deal of attention. By age four I could hardly wait for the Sunday paper. It came wrapped in several pages of colored comics. Charlotte would slowly read the words in the balloons above people's heads, and I eventually learned to read them with her. I loved to learn new words. I would play with them and make bad puns, sometimes in two languages.

We had a teenage babysitter. She invented games and played them with me. The one I loved most required her to overturn a high-backed easy chair. She made this a performance, with much grunting and groaning. I sat inside the arms and defended my castle against her attacks from all directions. I became fond of my babysitter and missed her greatly when we moved away.

2 The World Outside Our Yard

One of my earliest chores was to walk with Charlotte to the shopping area on Water Street, a few blocks away, where we bought a Yiddish daily newspaper for my father to read when he came home in the evening. We passed by a furniture factory that used banana oil (amyl acetate) in its varnish. The memory of its unique smell hasn't faded over the decades. A little farther down the street, fermented kosher dill pickles were made every day in large barrels. The area was bathed in a haze of dill and garlic that would make me salivate for a pastrami sandwich. I must have resembled an inquisitive puppy on our daily walks.

The kindergarten class that I attended at age five was boring. Its function was mostly babysitting. Apparently, educators at that time felt it was too soon to introduce books with words. I complained. I recall that my teacher felt that my social skills needed attention. I'm sure that I gave her reason to feel that way. Neither my teacher nor my classmates were of interest to me. I can't visualize any of them.

I improved socially at age six when my father bought a grocery store in another part of town, and we moved across the street from it. Our new neighborhood had broad ethnic diversity. School was now more interesting. I had a new friend, a classmate in first grade, whose family came from Canada and spoke French. When we played together in his home, they were enormously warm and friendly. I learned to say "comment ça va" in the local dialect instead of "hello" and assumed that I was simply adding to my vocabulary.

Worcester was the birthplace of Robert Goddard, the inventor of the liquid-fueled rocket. He conducted his early experiments in Auburn, only a few miles from where we lived. In 1926 my father had acquired his first car, a Model T Ford, and we drove in it to the initial test of Goddard's new rocket, a firing that had been pre-announced in the local paper. It was spectacular. It also made a lot of noise. It was objections to the noise from neighbors that eventually drove Goddard to Roswell and the surrounding New Mexico desert, well before the supposed arrival in Roswell of aliens from outer space. My early experience led to a continuing interest in Goddard and rockets. It seems more than a coincidence that, years later, I followed him to Worcester Polytechnic Institute and eventually, in 1983, received the Robert H. Goddard Award on the same campus.

I shared another interest with Goddard. He was a voracious reader and constantly visited the Worcester Public Library. As it happened, in our new home we lived about six blocks from the library. It offered fabulous possibilities. I went there almost every day, especially during school breaks. There was a children's side and an adult side that I was forbidden to enter. This was a problem. It got solved when my mother went with me and persuaded some official to grant me adult privileges. I quickly found a bookshelf full of the historical novels of Joseph Altsheler who wrote about American Indians, our colonial settlers, and our various early frontier wars. I became a devoted fan. Dickens and *Oliver Twist* came later.

Of course we celebrated the Fourth of July. There were almost no restrictions on the kinds of fireworks we set off in the streets. The explosions, the bursts of light, and the smell of gunpowder made the holiday unique and exciting. Following the Fourth, when I was seven or eight, I patrolled the neighborhood, picking up firecrackers that had failed to ignite, splitting them open, and examining their makeup. A burning fuse would heat the powder inside and make it explode. I held a lighted match to a little pile of the silvery powder. It flamed up and singed my hand.

The fireworks season was a good time to buy cans of grainy calcium carbide. When water was dripped on the grains, they generated a flammable gas, acetylene, used widely in lamps before battery-powered flashlights became common. Anyone could get calcium carbide, even kids. It had an unpleasant metallic smell, but it promised lots of fun.

We would put it under a can with a perforated lid, drip water through the hole, and then throw a lighted match at it. The acetylene and air mixture ignited with a loud explosion and blew the can high into the air. The fun stopped when some neighborhood boys poured a large amount of carbide into the corner street sewer and tossed in a burning match. Our street windows shattered. The boys were knocked to the ground and taken to the hospital in an ambulance. These days calcium carbide isn't easily available. Only spelunkers (cave explorers) seem to know where to buy it.

I found a job at age seven. The local bootlegger had access to a seemingly unlimited supply of grain alcohol and distributed it to people who made bathtub gin or colored it with caramelized sugar and sold it as whiskey. He worked out of an open touring car, packed in back with tins of alcohol. At his invitation, I joined him on his rounds and sat innocently in the car while he delivered his tins. I was given a quarter when he brought me back home. I'd earned only a couple of quarters when my mother asked me about my wealth. I no sooner told her than I was unemployed. I can't remember any sense of wrongdoing, only of economic hardship.

The Lindberg solo flight to Paris in 1927 lives on vividly in my brain. Newspapers in those times published "extras" that would suddenly flood the streets. I remember the extra with huge headlines announcing Lucky Lindy's arrival in Paris. The Lindy adoration that followed lasted for years. Model plane building became a craze. We could buy kits with sheets of balsa wood in Woolworth's. My ownership of a part interest in a real plane and a pilot's license had to wait almost thirty years after Lindy's flight.

Memorial Day was a big holiday. So was Armistice Day. We observed one minute of silence at 11 AM on November 11. Parades would fill Main Street on both these holidays. There were still marching and riding contingents of Civil War veterans wearing blue. Of course, there were also platoons of much younger World War I veterans. I don't remember any Rough Riders from the Spanish-American War, but I suppose there must have been a few. We put our caps over our hearts whenever the colors went by.

3 Movies and Vaudeville

We had no radio or TV in my early days, but movies were ubiquitous and were frequently combined with vaudeville. Although recorded sound tracks were yet to come, the movies were not really silent. Most theaters had, at the very least, a pianist who provided a live sound track. The major theaters had a trio or a small orchestra, particularly if the program also included a vaudeville show. They also had a newsreel and a "short," one of an ongoing series of episodes that invariably ended with an imminent catastrophe, the outcome to be resolved at the beginning of next week's installment.

Movies, at least once a week but usually more, were an essential part of our lives. They also served as babysitters for parents. Saturday at the movies became a must when my father started his grocery and meat market. Customers would phone in large orders that supplied not only Sunday dinners but also most of the week's less perishable needs. The orders were delivered by my father in his 1926 Model T Ford. While he was gone, my mother ran the store. We were given fifty cents and sent off to buy lunch and watch our heroes and heroines—Tom Mix, Hoot Gibson, Harold Lloyd, Charlie Chaplin, Douglas Fairbanks, Mary Pickford, and a helpless girl being tied to railroad tracks full of thundering freight trains.

My mother loved the movies. I was seven when she took me to watch *The Way of All Flesh,* starring the German movie star Emil Jannings. It was silent. The ending is etched in my mind. The once-happy and prosperous banker has been seduced and robbed of bank securities by a courtesan and thought to be dead. He has disappeared from society. Now he comes back in rags to the home of his abandoned family, creeps through the snow to peek into the living room window, and sees them all happily celebrating the holiday around a warm fireplace. My mother was audibly sobbing. I was, too. Jannings won an Academy Award for his role.

Sound arrived the same year. We stood in line at the Warner Theater to buy tickets to *The Jazz Singer* with Al Jolson. The orthodox father of the jazz singer wanted him to be a cantor, but he revolted. The intermittent sound track came on when he sang "Sonny Boy." The facial movements and sound weren't quite synchronized, but we hardly noticed. My sister bought the sheet music to play on the piano at home. I learned the lyrics and sang them often, complete with Jolson gestures.

The Palace (Poli) opened in 1926. It had three thousand seats and was built like a fairy-tale version of a palace, probably the grandest movie theater in New England. The performances included vaudeville by traveling Fanchon and Marco teams. It was there that I first saw Abbott and Costello do the "Who's on First" routine. I also remember Houdini, unbelievably draped in heavy chains and suspended upside down in a tank of water for interminable minutes. He suddenly emerged, carrying his chains. On another Saturday, the Singer Midgets cavorted mindlessly onstage until I almost left. The weekly backup line of sixteen long-legged chorines at the Palace was always spectacular.

4 Finding a Role

I began to serve customers in my father's meat market and grocery store at age eight. Often I would get up before sunrise and accompany him to the wholesale vegetable market and the walk-in meat freezer to buy supplies for the store. I learned what to look for in vegetables and how to choose sides of beef, pork, and lamb. He would stop at a diner for a cup of coffee and a frosted cruller. I got a doughnut. Sometimes we ran late and went hungry. The store had to open at 8 AM.

A waiting line of customers usually formed around five in the afternoon as people left work and shopped for their evening meals. I began to wait on them, pack bags, and add up the purchases. I would write the cost of each item on the side of the paper bag, add the column of figures, and present the total for payment. I learned to add by inspection, not as fast as today's supermarket checkout counters that read bar codes, but faster than punching numbers on a calculator.

I had to use our finger-threatening wheel-slicer constantly to fill orders for cheese and baloney, big sellers for sandwiches, particularly when the Great Depression hit the neighborhood. Men who had worked steadily for years at the big American Steel & Wire plant would pack their lunch boxes and go to the main gate of the mill, waiting to be called. Most of the time they would come back before noon, buy a bottle of pop at the store, and eat their sandwiches while sitting on the curb. Welfare checks became common, thirteen dollars a week for a family of four. The money was not supposed to be used to buy cigarettes, but sales remained high.

I was eight when I became involved in a presidential campaign. My teachers were all Catholics and clearly favored Al Smith, the first Catholic candidate, over Herbert Hoover. I wrote a little speech describing why I also approved of Al Smith. It was a tremendous hit with Alice Lee, my third-grade teacher, who sent me to all the other classrooms to campaign. I had no problem with being identified as a Democrat. Becoming an honorary Catholic was a little unsettling.

The same year at Christmastime I discovered the famous Gilbert chemistry set. I asked for one and was given the beginner's version. With it I got a general explanation of mysterious things going on around me, like painting iodine on wounds. These puzzling phenomena usually involved chemical reactions. I realized that chemistry was an important part of daily life.

I had a pure alto voice and became a member of an all-school choral group at age nine. Our most memorable concert involved an appearance at Worcester's Mechanics Hall, famous in the region for its acoustics. The featured artist was Percy Grainger. He predictably played "Country Gardens" on the piano and finished his concert with a series of compositions for musical glasses. He played them expertly. He may have chosen this instrument because he knew about the hall's acoustics. Each note was remarkably clear, almost harp-like. It was a great show.

Violin lessons and an hour's daily practice became a major activity for a while. My lessons stopped when the depression affected the family income. My mother explained that the violin was too demanding and was damaging my health. She was probably right. The violin is a maddening instrument in the hands of an impatient student. I took it up again as a teenager and played for a while with the high school orchestra but never mastered the instrument.

My eyesight deteriorated. I was amazed, at age ten, by the vividness of the world around me when I was first fitted with glasses. Perhaps it was my bad eyesight that encouraged my memory of odors. But now I could plainly see words and numbers on the blackboard at school. Books became even more interesting, and I continued to rush off to the public library when school was dismissed. I built a little tree house in the apple tree in our backyard and would climb up there with one hand while holding a book in the other. It was a favorite private retreat for several years.

Buck Rogers first appeared in the comics when I was ten. He was an immediate hit. I became an organizer of space flights on a front-porch rocket ship manned by a pickup crew of young neighbors. Although the notion of flying in space had already been introduced by H. G. Wells, Jules Verne, Goddard, and others, our big hero was Buck Rogers. I was his self-appointed local representative.

I became interested in public radio. It was growing rapidly. A low-power station, WTAG, had opened in Worcester. KDKA was a powerful station at the Pittsburgh headquarters of Westinghouse. Its signal could be picked up in Massachusetts. In 1930 I had a new close friend, Charlie Schon, who occasionally spoke Swedish when at home with his immigrant mother. There were just the two of them living in a one-room flat. At his suggestion we built a poor man's radio, a "crystal" set. It was named after the small piece of lead sulfide that was needed as a detector. The tuner was a copper coil that we wound around the cardboard tube from a roll of toilet paper. We needed copper wire for the coil and over 60 feet of additional wire for a long antenna and for grounding the crystal. The last part was the earphone that was provided by an old, discarded telephone. It was exciting to install the antenna. It had to be attached high up on the house next door and brought in through the second-floor window. It was even more thrilling to move a "tickler" wire across the coil, completing a tuned circuit to the earphone. Suddenly we heard WTAG. The price of vacuum-tube radios, which amplified the signal enough to drive a loudspeaker, had now become low enough so that we had one in our living room and constantly listened to it. The crystal set remained with Charlie. He later became a radio announcer and then a TV commentator.

5 The Deepening Depression

My father was increasingly concerned as unpaid bills of our customers ran up. His own debts to suppliers increased. But he never refused food to people who came in hungry. The standard issue was a few thin slices of baloney between two slices of sandwich bread dabbed with mustard. I made some nearly every day.

Banks began to fail. Unemployed veterans gathered in Washington in the summer of 1932 and demanded payment of the bonuses that had been promised them. Their encampment was attacked and burned out by troops commanded by General Douglas MacArthur. We began to hear talk about a national uprising led by radical Communists. My parents were more conservative and favored the Socialists. President Hoover was widely blamed and lost to Franklin Roosevelt by a landslide in the 1932 election.

The deepening depression didn't interfere with plans for an elaborate thirteenth birthday ceremony in February, the Bar Mitzvah of the oldest son. I had no religious sense, no conviction that anyone was listening to the Hebrew prayers I was reciting other than my teacher and my parents. The overriding need was to make no mistakes in the incantation of the prescribed passages of Torah. The formalities at the Saturday service were followed by a big party at a rented hall in Boston. I was required to make a speech. It was a ritual. In return the guests congratulated me, each and every one separately, and handed me cash gifts. A rich uncle gave me a twenty-dollar gold piece. I dutifully handed fistfuls of paper bills to my mother. My parents obviously loved it all. I recall a sense of great pressure and duty.

We were living in an increasingly grim world. Two weeks earlier Hitler had been appointed chancellor of Germany. Two weeks after my party, the Reichstag burned to the ground. Hitler assumed the role of Übermensch, and the transformation of Germany to the terror of the Third Reich began.

On March 4 most radios turned to the broadcast of Roosevelt's maiden inaugural speech. His first job was to restore confidence in our government. This was how he began:

> I am certain that my fellow Americans expect that on my induction into the Presidency I will address them with a candor and a decision which the present situation of our Nation impels. This is preeminently the time to speak the truth, the whole truth, frankly and boldly. Nor need we shrink from honestly facing conditions in our country today. This great Nation will endure as it has endured, will revive and will prosper. So, first of all, let me assert my firm belief that the only thing we have to fear is fear itself—nameless, unreasoning, unjustified terror which paralyzes needed efforts to convert retreat into advance. In every dark hour of our national life a leadership of frankness and vigor has met with that understanding and support of the people themselves that is essential to victory. I am convinced that you will again give that support to leadership in these critical days.

Like many millions of listeners in his audience that day, I was captivated by FDR's words, voice, and style and became a devoted fan. His administration began boldly. A financial panic had caused the failure of over ten thousand banks under the Hoover administration, and fear among depositors was turning to panic. On March 5, the day after his inauguration, he announced a bank holiday. All banks were closed. Caught without cash, people began to write IOU's rather than checks. The cash register at our store began to fill with signed notes. On March 19, solvent banks were allowed to reopen. The panic subsided.

6 My High School Years

My mother died in 1934 of peritonitis following minor surgery. It was before the days of antibiotics. She had gone to a surgeon who operated a private hospital only a few blocks from the store because she knew that my father could visit her without taking too much time away from work. She had great respect for doctors and was not sophisticated about the practice of medicine by unaccredited physicians in unaccredited hospitals. Her death left me bitter and angry. We had a string of housekeepers until my father remarried in 1936. I was largely on my own. Self-discipline was not one of my strengths, and I lost much of the focus that she had nurtured.

I began to visit the Worcester *Telegram and Gazette* plant regularly. The city editor was a customer at the store. He was a steak lover and favored the first cut off the sirloin, one and one-half inches thick. My visits to modern supermarkets constantly remind me that I used to cut all meat with a sharp knife and severed bones with a meat ax, not a band saw. I am now often tempted to go back into the freezer room at our supermarket and cut my own lamb chops, down the ribs and not across them.

I suppose the fact that I did custom butchery for the editor helped to gain access to the newspaper. I had been sending little essays and drawings to the Sunday edition's children's page. Whenever anything was accepted for publication, I got a dollar bill. It was thrilling and profitable to see my words and art in print. I wanted to know more about the whole process.

All the newspaper's employees were friendly and explained what they were doing. I started with the newsroom where the stories got typed and the pages composed. I also visited the photoengraving shop where they transferred photos to metal plates for the printing press. The political cartoonist was fascinating and would give me yesterday's board to take home. I went down to the linotype room where operators typed text and turned each line into a metal slug that locked into the printing press roller. I would be given a slug with my name on it, a highly prized souvenir. Then I was allowed to enter the impressive, noisy printing press room where the actual paper got produced and sent in stacks to the waiting trucks. I began to think about becoming a newspaperman.

My fascination with publishing led me to join the editorial board of the Classical High School student newspaper. I also enjoyed singing with the glee club for two years but eventually gave up trying to remain a tenor. In my junior year, attracted by an income of a few dollars a week, I took the job of high school gossip columnist on a weekly paper and reviewed as many parties and romantic attachments, real and imagined, as I could find out about. I used the name "Sinthia" and remained anonymous for a year.

Pretty girls were increasingly interesting. Classical High School seemed to have more than its share of them. I fell suddenly in love with beautiful, sylphlike Sylvia. It happened when I took her on a first date to watch Fred Astaire and Ginger Rogers in the movie *Swing Time*. Fred serenaded Ginger with "The Way You Look Tonight." I looked fondly at Sylvia. She looked back. It was the beginning of a high school romance that lasted until she went away to college and soon found someone else. I was devastated.

My interest in science continued. I pursued the intellectual aspects mostly with books checked out of the public library. Classical High School paid more attention to Latin, Greek, and history than to physics and chemistry. However, my biology class was excellent. We worked with frogs. It was fun to learn that leg muscles could be activated electrically. Their fibers twitched with the slightest stimulus.

I also enjoyed debating and participated in a number of meetings with teams from other high schools. Conversations with fellow debaters, usually on social or political topics, were even more enjoyable than the debates. I served as president of the society in my senior year.

In my high school sophomore year I joined the local chapter of a national high school fraternity and formed a close friendship with Harold Pines, one of the members. His father had a cigar factory that employed immigrants from Cuba who faithfully made Havana-type cigars. Mr. Pines always had one firmly clenched on the right side of his mouth. He was short and stocky and made large cigars look even larger.

Hal's mother liked to entertain interesting people at dinner, and I felt greatly honored when I was occasionally seated at the foot of the table. I particularly remember the night I met Gregory Pincus. He was doing controversial research at Harvard and then, having been denied tenure, joined Clark University in Worcester. He was learning how to control pregnancy in female rabbits. He talked about the possibility of developing a birth control pill for humans. Later, his work attracted the attention of Margaret Sanger, probably the major advocate of birth control in the United States. It was not a standard academic subject. Contraception was illegal in Massachusetts. Pincus later became cofounder of the Worcester Foundation for Experimental Biology and an acknowledged leader in the development of oral contraceptives.

During Christmas week, 1936, I attended a fraternity convention in New York City and splurged on a trip to the Metropolitan Opera. The performance was Wagner's *Tristan and Isolde,* with opera legends Lauritz Melchior and Kirsten Flagstad in the starring roles. I didn't know that it lasted five hours and was less enthused about this historic performance than I should have been. It was several years before I attended another opera.

My fondness for jazz took me to the Cotton Club in Harlem. I was with a New York sophisticate, my age but much more worldly. No one questioned our ages when we ordered drinks, even after I fell to the floor while attempting to boogie. I also saw a performance of Cole Porter's new musical comedy *Red, Hot and Blue!* with Jimmy Durante and Ethel Merman. A third star was a person I had never heard of until then, Bob Hope.

Later that week I had dinner at the 21 Club, formerly known as Jack and Charlie's, New York's famous and exclusive speakeasy during Prohibition. Jack Kreindler, co-owner of the club, was an alumnus of the fraternity. He closed the restaurant for the night to treat the high school members and adult mentors to great food and appearances by a string of Broadway celebrities. Unlike the other restaurants I had visited, the 21 Club did not allow teenagers to order alcohol.

7 Undergraduate Years at Worcester Polytechnic Institute

Without knowing how I could pay my tuition, I applied for admission to Harvard but was rejected. However, I was offered scholarships at MIT and WPI. Even with MIT's help, I would have needed to go into debt to live in Cambridge. I chose WPI and decided to major in chemistry. Engineering courses were compulsory and proved to be valuable in later life. English and literature classes were weak. I felt that English was a major gap in the curriculum. It helped to join the school debating club and eventually chair it. It was one of my most interesting and valuable undergraduate activities.

I was not first-rate in the laboratory. I slowly and painfully learned to be scrupulously attentive to tiny details. In 1939 an assignment in bacteriology lab led to the shutdown of a major dairy in Worcester County. My task was to culture any bacterial colony that could be isolated from groundwater or milk. I used milk and got an unrecognizable growth in my Petri dish. The bacteriology professor quickly identified it as brucella abortus, a bacterium that produces undulant fever in cows and causes them to abort their calves. The dairy that provided the milk had to stop production and revaccinate its herd.

Despite the sweeping measures of Roosevelt's New Deal, the Great Depression continued. Even though room and board at home were free, I spent much of my time earning badly needed cash. I worked constantly at odd jobs around campus, sold women's shoes downtown, and went door-to-door one summer peddling encyclopedias. My friends were modestly wealthy by the standards of the day, but I had to scramble for pocket money.

The administration of Worcester Polytechnic Institute was rabidly Republican. In my sophomore year we were visited by Joseph Pew, head of the Sun Oil Company. He gave a fiercely anti–New Deal, anti-Roosevelt talk to the student body. I was a reporter on the campus newspaper and covered the event. My account was not favorable. My term on the newspaper staff quickly ended.

I became interested in the importance of Mr. Pew's company in world affairs. I composed an essay that dealt with the vital need for oil in the growing confrontation between Hitler's Germany and opposing European powers. Germany had no oil fields. Its tanks and air force had to depend on petroleum imports and, increasingly, on the catalytic Fischer-Tropsch process to make petroleum. The essay described the Bergius process for synthesizing liquid fuel from coal and the Houdry process for catalytically cracking heavy oil residues. The latter invention doubled the yield of high-grade gasoline at the Sun Oil Company and added greatly to Mr. Pew's wealth. I predicted that Houdry, who had come to the United States in 1931 to work with the Vacuum Oil Company, would become a crucially important asset in case of war. Sun Oil and Socony-Vacuum joined forces, and Sun opened the first big Houdry process plant in 1937. It revolutionized the industry.

I speculated that if Hitler went to war, he would first turn east to guarantee an oil supply, probably from the fields in Romania and Hungary. This is substantially what happened. Hitler began World War II with the invasion of Poland in September 1939. Romania officially joined Germany in the war in November 1940 and became a major supplier of oil. Much of my speculation was based on what I had learned in chemistry and chemical engineering classes. The essay won a fifty-dollar award in a campus contest and made me prosperous for several months.

My undergraduate academic record was not distinguished. Girls and weekend dating seemed more important at the time. I began to smoke cigarettes and puffed on a Kaywoodie pipe that I didn't particularly enjoy. My eyeglasses were old and not properly corrected. It hurt to read. I cut down on the time I spent with books and neglected required but unappealing courses. I remained an avid newspaper reader, a habit that eventually brought me to Princeton.

In early 1939, when I was taking a sophomore physics course at Worcester Polytechnic Institute, I found a newspaper story about the discovery of fission in uranium. I clipped it out and brought it to my physics professor. Disagreeing with the speculation in the article, Professor Morton Masius felt that a chain reaction was unlikely. He apparently assumed that the number of neutrons released per fission was lower than was actually the case.

8 Entering a New World

When I completed my undergraduate work and was waiting to see if I would be drafted into the army, Professor Masius remembered my interest in fission and suggested that I talk with his friend at Princeton, Professor Eugene Wigner. Although the work of the Wigner group was not described, I am sure that Professor Masius knew exactly what they were doing. I hitchhiked to Princeton for an interview with Professor Wigner. At the end of the afternoon he invited me to join his group. I immediately accepted.

I was now in a secret world. Shortly after I had raised the subject of fission with Professor Masius in 1939, a number of prominent scientists became strangely silent about their work. They had realized that the devastating atomic bomb of fiction might now become a reality. Six months after the discovery of fission Einstein was visited, first by refugee Hungarian physicists Leo Szilard and Eugene Wigner, and later by Szilard and Hungarian physicist Edward Teller. They were concerned that Germany might be well on the way toward developing an atomic bomb. Einstein eventually signed a letter to President Roosevelt concerning the terrible threat to the United States if Germany were to be successful. The letter initially produced minimal funding for research on the design of a chain reaction in a natural uranium pile proposed by Szilard and Enrico Fermi, who had fled Italy because he had a Jewish wife. Hitler's war against Jews and Mussolini's imitative policies in Italy had deprived their countries of many of their most brilliant scientists, who now dedicated themselves to the defeat of the Fascists.

For the next nearly three years Fermi and Szilard at Columbia University, together with Wigner at Princeton and Teller at George Washington University, were major figures in nuclear research on the East Coast of the United States. They pursued the design of a chain-reacting pile. A second group at Columbia University, headed by Harold Urey and John Dunning, focused on separation of highly fissionable uranium-235 from uranium-238 by diffusion of gaseous uranium hexafluoride through porous barriers. On the West Coast, a group headed by E. O. Lawrence at Berkeley concentrated on separating the highly fissionable uranium isotope of mass 235 from mass 238 by separation of ionized atoms in a magnetic field.

What was then known was that uranium-238, the heavy uranium isotope, is over 99 percent abundant in natural uranium. It does not undergo fission when it captures a slow neutron but becomes radioactive mass 239 that decays by emitting an electron (a beta particle) to become neptunium-239. The major fissionable isotope in uranium is the less than 1 percent abundant isotope of mass 235. It has a very large tendency to capture slow neutrons and to fission, splitting into two lighter atoms that range widely in mass across the middle of the periodic table of the elements. When it fissions, it also emits gamma rays and two or three very energetic neutrons. They collide with neighboring atoms and then escape to the air or produce new fissions in uranium-235 or get captured in uranium-238 to make uranium-239, which then decays to neptunium and then to plutonium.

Not known to Szilard and Fermi was whether at least one of the neutrons produced in fission would cause another fission in uranium-235. In practical terms this meant that, on average, uranium-238 could not capture more than one and one-half neutrons per fission. To design the reactor it was necessary to minimize the capture of energetic neutrons over the whole history of their slowing down to thermal energy in the graphite moderator. If the number of neutrons captured per fission was more than one and one-half, a natural chain reactor would be impossible. If it was smaller, the building of a chain reactor could go full speed ahead. Of course, neutron capture in impurities could also doom a chain reactor, but it was assumed that the impurities could be removed.

The Berkeley scientists concentrated on methods for separating the rare fissionable isotope uranium-235 from the abundant but relatively useless uranium-238. If successful, the concentrated uranium-235 could be easily fabricated into a nuclear bomb. However, even the most optimistic estimates indicated that the amount of separated material needed to make a bomb would be at least 50 kilograms, over 100 pounds. It would take an enormous industrial effort to succeed.

There were a number of options for separating isotopes of the same element. Two of them were favored. One was gaseous diffusion. It depended on the fact that, in gas form, the lighter isotope travels slightly faster through porous barriers than the heavier isotope. The second method depended on ionizing the isotopes, accelerating them, and bending their paths in a strong magnetic field. Uranium-235 would follow a more highly curved path than uranium-238 and could be collected in its own trap. A third option, the gas centrifuge, was abandoned because it required construction with high-strength, chemically inert metal alloys that were not yet developed. In retrospect, it was the most promising option and should have been pursued. It is now the method of choice for enriching uranium-235.

When I joined the Princeton group in the fall of 1941, government support was rapidly accelerating, spurred by optimistic predictions of success from U.S. panels of experts and some equally dedicated groups in Great Britain. As in the United States, the British group was greatly strengthened by a number of refugees from Germany and France. Optimism was tempered by a growing conviction that the Germans were also moving rapidly ahead and the fear that Hitler might get an atomic bomb first. There was little doubt that the first country to succeed would win the war. Fear of losing to the monstrous Hitler erased any serious thought of rejecting development of a bomb on moral grounds.

Everyone who knew him has a Feynman story. I met Dick Feynman on my first day at work. I had been assigned to a very small office in the basement of the Palmer Physics Building, close to the cyclotron. I sat at a bare desk with only a telephone on it and stared at the empty shelves, estimating how many feet of books I would want to ship from home. Someone burst into the room, a rather tall, slim person with swept-back black hair. He stopped, obviously not expecting to find the room occupied. Then he said, "May I use your phone?" I nodded. He whipped out a little screwdriver, quickly disassembled the phone, and left with a piece of it in his hand.

That evening I went to an eating club for my first after-work meal. When I sat down, I recognized the person sitting on the opposite side as my office visitor. I said, "Are you through using my phone?" He looked a little embarrassed and said, "I'll take care of that," and introduced himself. I recognized the name. It was the same as the name on a sign posted on the door to the cyclotron control room. The sign said, "Don't let Dick Feynman in. He takes tools."

The next day Dick came back, produced the missing piece, reassembled the phone, and made sure that it worked. My subsequent meetings with him were more social and tutorial. I learned about his ill girlfriend back home. He told me how a timeless excursion through the quantum vacuum of a single, unimaginably energetic "thing" would leave a trail of particles that could eventually make a universe. Talking with Dick introduced me to a world I could never have otherwise imagined. He made my mind work harder than ever before.

9 Prologue to the Manhattan Project

It was still a year before the Manhattan Project came into being under General Groves. In the interim, secrecy was entirely voluntary on the part of the research scientists at Princeton, Columbia, and Berkeley. At Princeton the secrecy was at first concerned with the answer to the big question: could a fission chain reaction be achieved with natural uranium? The importance of the reactor greatly increased in 1941 with the discovery at Berkeley of plutonium-239. It is even more fissionable than uranium-235. It could be made in quantity in a reactor by the capture of neutrons in uranium-238 followed by the decay of uranium-239 and neptunium-239 to plutonium-239. Plutonium could be separated from uranium chemically. This path to the bomb began to look easier than the separation of uranium-235 from uranium-238.

My group bombarded uranium targets at the cyclotron, separated the uranium from all of its fission products, and counted the beta particles emitted by the capture product uranium-239. It decayed with a half-life of 24 minutes, so the chemical processing and counting had to be done quickly. The target was dissolved in nitric acid to make uranyl nitrate. It had the unusual property of being very soluble in ethyl ether, entirely unlike the nitrates of other metallic elements. We quickly extracted the uranyl nitrate, separating it from a multitude of other radioactive products, burned off the highly flammable ether, ignited the nitrate to uranium oxide, mounted it on a small slide, and counted the decay particles in a beta counter. This had to be done many times under a variety of conditions. I made a contribution to the process by adding a solid, water-absorbent Drierite to the ether. My modified procedure reduced contaminating fission products by a factor of ten and greatly improved the accuracy of our results. I felt that I had arrived as a professional chemist.

We had to repeat our measurements at very high moderator temperatures to see how much the capture cross-section of uranium changed as the neutrons got hotter. A Globar furnace, fitted around the moderating graphite column, provided neutrons with energies corresponding to a temperature of 1000 degrees C. Unfortunately, the outer surface layer of graphite oxidized to carbon monoxide at this temperature. We discovered this problem when I passed out while recovering a target. Ed Creutz, my supervisor, installed fans in the area to minimize the carbon monoxide concentration and then bought a canary from a Princeton pet shop and installed it in a cage set in the target area. Canaries are used in coal mines because they fall unconscious when carbon monoxide levels get dangerously high. Being a careful experimentalist, Ed decided that we had to calibrate our canary. We threw a big tarp over the cage and put an electric light on an extension cord under the tarp. Then we added a long rubber tube, attached at one end to a Bunsen burner gas valve. When all was ready, Ed turned on the light, got under the tarp and I opened the gas valve. After a few minutes, he flung off the tarp with a cry of triumph. The canary was lying motionless on the bottom of the cage. After a while it revived and began to sing. It became a cheerful addition to the cyclotron crew.

Once our job was done with uranium oxide targets, it had to be done again with uranium metal targets to separate out the effect of the oxygen. But we didn't have a good source of uranium metal. The only supplier was a firm called Metal Hydrides in Beverly, Massachusetts. Its product was a finely divided powder that caught fire the moment it was exposed to air. We ordered what they had, something over a kilogram. I drove with a colleague to Beverly in an open-air convertible. Once there, we had to transfer the powder under a layer of dry ice to a sturdy can, seal the can, and drive back to Princeton. During the trip I sat on the passenger side with the can covered with dry ice in a small tub between my legs. I planned to kick it all out on the road if it caught fire. Once back at the lab, we opened the can. The moment a few particles of the powder were dislodged, everything caught fire.

We threw the whole tub out on the adjacent lawn and watched a spectacular show as the can sank into the melting soil.

The next day Professor Wigner asked me to find another source of uranium metal. After some hours in the library, I came back with the news that two people at Westinghouse, Marden and Rentschler, had made pure uranium metal for lamp filaments at the Westinghouse plant in Bloomfield, New Jersey. They held a patent on the process. Bloomfield was just outside New York City, only fifty miles away.

Ed Creutz went to Bloomfield only days later and was remarkably persuasive. Westinghouse soon found itself committed to delivering enough uranium metal to make many, many lamp filaments. It was the beginning of their rapidly growing role as a major supplier to the Manhattan Project.

Professor Wigner and our group received many interesting visitors. In addition to Enrico Fermi, Leo Szilard, and Edward Teller, I particularly remember a visit by Hans von Halban, an associate of Frederic Joliot at the Curie Institute in Paris. He was a pioneer in research with neutrons and in the investigation of fission in uranium. Only months after the discovery of fission, he and three associates filed three patents involving designs for a chain-reacting configuration of natural uranium, the first patents ever issued on a uranium reactor. The choice of a neutron moderator was all-important. They rejected the use of normal hydrogen and, unlike Szilard and Fermi, concluded that graphite was unsuitable. They eventually chose "heavy" water, made with hydrogen of mass two, deuterium, and by late 1939 concluded that uranium oxide, suspended in heavy water, would indeed sustain a chain reaction.

Norsk Hydro, a firm located in Norway, was the only source of heavy water in quantity. Using cheap hydroelectricity, the company had made 185 kg. The French negotiated for use of the entire stock, and on March 9, 1940, a mission went to Norway and brought back all the precious moderator in twenty-six cans. It was just two months before the Battle of France and three months before the fall of Paris. By then, the French government had fled to Bordeaux.

During his visit I had a conversation with von Halban, an extremely open and pleasant person. He told me that, as the Germans advanced on Paris, he had packed the back of an open touring car with the very secret cans of heavy water, put cushions over the cans, spread blankets over the cushions, sat his children on the blankets, told them always to look happy, and took off for Bordeaux. It reminded me of my experience as a bootlegger at age seven. The smiling family group managed to pass several checkpoints en route and eventually reached Bordeaux where they met coworker Leo Kowarski and were loaded aboard a freighter that took them to England. They joined the staff at the Chadwick Laboratory and used the heavy water to demonstrate conclusively that their design would work. However, a chain reactor would take about thirty times as much moderator as they had on hand. A fictionalized version of his escape to England is part of the plot of a 2003 French movie, *Bon Voyage.*

The Manhattan Project later undertook the production of the necessary amount of heavy water. It was used to construct the first successful reactor prototype at Argonne, Illinois, in May 1944. The design behaved much as von Halban had predicted a few months after the discovery of fission.

10 I Go to the "Met Lab"

In the spring of 1942 I moved with my Princeton group to the University of Chicago's new Metallurgical Laboratory (Met Lab), the center for construction of the Fermi pile at the university's football stadium, Stagg Field, and for plutonium research. I joined the Fermi group. The need for large quantities of pure uranium was greater than ever, and I was soon sent to the Mallinckrodt Company in St. Louis to help start a production plant that was beginning to extract tons of uranyl nitrate into ether. The nitrate was then converted to uranium oxide. The process was the same as the one I had helped develop at Princeton but on an industrial scale. The plumbing was full of ether fumes that occasionally exploded, sending sheets of fire out of all the sinks. But Jack Kyger, the brilliant young MIT engineer in charge of the project, worked around the clock, solving the startup problems and getting the plant to full capacity within a month. Once the plant was running properly I was told to return to Chicago. Jack and I continued to get together for dinner dates on his occasional visits to Chicago.

My supervisor at the Met Lab was Herbert Anderson, Fermi's right-hand man. He required a neutron source to measure reactivity of the Fermi pile. Neutron sources were usually made with a mixture of radium and beryllium. The alpha particles emitted by radium hit the beryllium and made neutrons. The sources were prepared by drying a solution of radium on beryllium metal powder and sealing the mixture in a leak-proof brass capsule. I was coached on what to do and sent to New York carrying beryllium powder, a brass capsule, and a gamma survey meter to make sure that once the capsule was soldered shut, it didn't leak radioactive radon. We didn't know it at the time, but the danger posed by the beryllium was greater than the potential damage from radiation. Herb Anderson eventually died of berylliosis, a lung disease caused by breathing beryllium or beryllium oxide.

I traveled by train to New York and took a cab to a big building on Sixth Avenue that housed the offices of Radium Chemical Company. I brought a portable survey meter with me that measured gamma radiation. It started to register when I entered the building. It went berserk when I checked out the primitive chemical hood I was directed to use to make the neutron source. Out of a mixture of curiosity and alarm I took the elevator to the rooftop. Air from the hood was discharged there. Even by the loose standards we used at that time, the roof was unacceptably radioactive. The gamma radiation level was higher than anything I had ever encountered in a public environment.

I spent two days at the Radium Chemical Company making and checking the neutron source. I was anxious to leave as soon as possible. Coming from the Manhattan Project, I could make no comment that would attract attention. I later found that the owners of the company had operated under a different name in New Jersey, where they employed young women to paint luminous watch dials with radium-loaded brushes which they tipped with their mouths. Several died of radiation-induced bone cancers. The owners moved to Manhattan and, after the war, to Queens. The building that the company occupied there wasn't identified as a radiation hazard until 1983. The company was finally ordered to shut down completely in the late 1980s and the building was demolished.

I think of the Radium Chemical Company whenever I hear or read that the Manhattan Project and its successors exposed the general public to hazardous levels of contamination. This statement is most frequently made by people who define the word "hazardous" as arising from any increment to the natural background level, however small. But before the Manhattan Project came into being, the public was routinely exposed to relatively high levels of radiation from a wide variety of sources. For example, in the 1930s, shoes were frequently fitted for size by examination of the foot in a fluoroscope with an attendant heavy dose of X-rays. Acne in teenagers was frequently treated with large doses of soft X-rays. Many young people developed horribly disfigured faces as adults. Dental and medical X-rays were major sources. Most people owned radiant dial alarm clocks and many wore luminous wrist-watches. I suspect that increased public awareness of radiation has, in fact, helped reduce the lifetime exposures of many millions of people. The list of easily overlooked sources is long. Some of them still remain generally unrecognized.

When I returned to Chicago I joined my colleagues in the machining of graphite into blocks that were used in the construction of the Fermi pile. Ultra-pure graphitic carbon was the element of choice in the Fermi-Szilard design because it scattered and slowed down fission neutrons without absorbing very many. The need for uranium metal to insert in the center of the pile became a top priority, and I was sent to MIT to expedite production. I was happy to do this and escape from the graphite-machining crew that made everyone look like performers in a nineteenth-century minstrel show.

The Department of Metallurgy at MIT was receiving shipments of the infamous, spontaneously flammable Metal Hydrides powdered uranium metal. They were taught to carefully transfer the powder, protected by chunks of dry ice, to a high-powered vacuum induction furnace. There it was supposed to be melted, cast into rods, sawed into cylinders of equal length and diameter, and shipped to Chicago. But there were problems. When power to the induction furnace was turned on, the vacuum would suddenly be broken and the power would turn off. Working with a desktop model of the furnace, I found that the temperature of the furnace had to be raised slowly to allow the film of ice that had condensed on each cold grain from the humid New England atmosphere to totally evaporate. Otherwise the furnace temperature went by the boiling point of water so quickly that the ice exploded.

Once the supply of cast metal rods was assured, a production bottleneck occurred in the machine shop set up next door to saw the rods into right cylinders. High-grade diamond saws were required. They were expensive. Our very experienced machinist fed the rods through the saws in a way that maximized the number of cuts per saw but also made the feed rate painfully slow. With authorization from Chicago, I bought up the entire local supply of diamond saws and told the machinist to greatly increase the feed rate. Protesting loudly, he did this until he was spending almost as much time replacing saws as sawing. But the bottleneck disappeared.

One day I was suddenly called into the machine shop. A bucket of uranium metal chips from the sawing process had caught fire. The fire extinguishers hanging on the corridor walls were a trademarked brand called "Pyrene." They contained breakable glass containers filled with carbon tetrachloride. I was afraid that if carbon tetrachloride were oxidized at the very high temperature of burning uranium metal, it would become carbonyl dichloride, commonly known as phosgene. I was familiar with the use of phosgene as a poison gas on the battle-fields of World War I. We found buckets of sand and put out the fire. I then went to the library and discovered that we had, indeed, avoided making phosgene.

I avoided another disaster in the Boston area by not being there. A friend and I passed a popular nightclub in downtown Boston on Saturday night, November 28. People were being turned away because it was overcrowded. The next morning we learned that 492 people had died later that evening in the Cocoanut [sic] Grove fire.

We shipped our uranium ingots in boxes labeled "Titanium." The density of titanium is about one-fourth that of uranium. When two of us would painfully lift the relatively small boxes of "Titanium" into the back of a station wagon in the alley next to the Metallurgy Department, the bright students who watched our knees buckle and the wagon sag on its springs with each load must certainly have known that the boxes contained something much heavier than titanium.

On December 2, 1942, the Fermi reactor went critical. Immediately afterward I was called back to Chicago. I felt that my mission at MIT had deprived me of being present at a unique moment in history at Stagg Field. I wish I had been there.

I remained in Chicago for a year without any more sudden, out-of-town assignments. People from DuPont had joined us and were on call for a variety of production problems. Some of my old colleagues were drafted to go to the new laboratory at Oak Ridge. I left the physics group and worked in the newly constructed chemistry lab, referred to as New Chem, where I explored innovative ways to separate pluto-nium from uranium solutions. The most promising method involved an organic complex of plutonium, a type of compound called a che-late, which I extracted into chloroform, deposited on a platinum plate, and assayed by counting the rate of emission of alpha particles.

Glenn Seaborg, the codiscoverer of plutonium-239, was now in charge of most plutonium research at the Met Lab. He was located just down the hall from my lab. His task was to design the plutonium separation process that would be used at Hanford, about to become the major plutonium producer. I suggested to him that solvent extraction of a plutonium chelate might be a candidate for chemical separation. He said that any organic compound would be unstable in the very high radiation fields produced by irradiated fuel rods. The methods of choice for Hanford would be either co-precipitation of plutonium on lanthanum fluoride or bismuth phosphate. The final choice of bismuth phosphate, named the BiPO process, was made by DuPont's Crawford Greenewalt.

My lab mate at New Chem was Mark Goldsmith, a sophisticated character with a sardonic sense of humor. He liked to identify himself on answering the phone with the names of various celebrities. If the call was for me, I would have to explain that I wasn't entertaining Gary Cooper or being interviewed by Walter Winchell.

Mark's work involved extraction of uranyl nitrate into ethyl ether. He recovered the ether on a distillation column, unaware that unstable ether peroxides were building up in his solvent. The column was busily bubbling one afternoon when it exploded with a thundering blast. I unglued myself from a desk seat and tried to pull open the door leading to an outside corridor. It was tilted out and jammed. Framed in the door window on the corridor side was a famous face, a person whose name Mark might have used in answering the phone. It was James Bryant Conant, president of Harvard, who was visiting the lab and had been about to come in and talk with me. He was tugging on the door from the other side.

I looked around. Mark was pulling himself together on one side of the room. The other side was a wall that faced onto a back alley. It was now leaning into the alley with a gap big enough to squeeze through. I ran through the alley and back to the guarded front door, explained to the guard that my pass had been left inside, and raced down the corridor to my lab. A crowd had assembled and people were helping President Conant pull the door open. They succeeded and my shaken colleague emerged. We both went to first aid. Damage was limited to minor burns.

11 My Visit to Oak Ridge

In early 1944 Site X-10 at Oak Ridge began to produce plutonium in its new reactor in amounts much greater than previously available from cyclotron bombardments. We received enough at Chicago to see its attractive blue and pink colors in trivalent and tetravalent oxidation states. The production people at Oak Ridge did not trust their varying assay results and asked for some expert at Chicago to come down and referee their analytical methods. I was told to pack my bags and leave for Oak Ridge.

My friends at Oak Ridge heard I was coming down. I began to receive urgent phone calls. They all said the same thing, "Bring gin and whiskey." Oak Ridge was in a dry county and liquor had to be bought from bootleggers at inflated prices. It took me back to my childhood days.

I spent several hours patrolling liquor stores on 63rd Street and packed my purchases in a large suitcase. I paid a redcap to haul my bags to my Pullman car to Knoxville. I found my place and discovered that my seatmate was the director of Met Lab, Arthur Holly Compton. He was making a trip to Oak Ridge to attend a suddenly called meeting. Unlike me, he had no berth for the night and planned to sit up. I offered him my berth but he refused.

The next morning he told me that the train would make a special stop at Elza Crossing, short of Knoxville, and that I should get off there with him and share his ride to Oak Ridge. As we started to get off the train, he picked up one of my two bags. It was the one packed with liquor, very heavy and loudly gurgling. He insisted on carrying it and helping with great care to put it into the waiting car.

I was dropped off at what looked like a hastily constructed Army barracks, a cemestos-walled, boxy building. It was not a warm welcome to Oak Ridge. Next morning I joined large crowds at a central loading point to take a bus to X-10. Other buses loaded workers going to K-25, the gaseous diffusion plant, and Y-12, the electromagnetic isotope separation plant. Conversation on the bus was loud and communal, mostly about the latest titillating scandals reported in the local newspaper's gossip column.

I had packed lightly and needed a clean white shirt for a party that evening. There was no place in Oak Ridge to buy one, but I was told a men's store existed in a nearby town. I borrowed a car and, following directions, was soon on a muddy main street lined with shabby storefronts. One store stood out. It was freshly painted, the very place I was looking for. I went in and was greeted warmly by the proprietor. His accent told me that his first language was Yiddish and his second New York Brooklynese. I stared at him and said, "What are you doing here?" He replied, "My truck broke down." He went on to explain that he didn't have enough money to repair the truck and began to sell his inventory in town. Business was unexpectedly brisk, due mostly to the exploding population at Oak Ridge. He decided to stay, rented a store, bought furniture and more inventory, and quickly became the major business in town. "God was good to me," he said. I nodded, thinking that General Groves, if fitted with a white beard, would, indeed, have a certain resemblance to the conventional versions of Jehovah.

My draft board in Worcester was a faithful correspondent during much of the war. It had classified me 1-A in 1942. This meant I had to go periodically to the nearest army examining office to report for duty. My employers would appeal each time I was scheduled to be drafted and I would be granted a temporary exemption. After several such exemptions, in 1944 the draft board sent me a copy of a permanent exemption from the Office of the President with an exclamation mark in red ink after the line that identified the president. The exemption arrived after I had reported for full examination by an army physician and an army psychiatrist in downtown Chicago. It was the last time I heard from my draft board. Almost all of my old friends were in military service. I felt some guilt about not being with them. I was unable to explain why I continued to be a civilian.

If I had been drafted, I would have been put in uniform and sent back to some part of the Manhattan Project. Many other young men were assigned to what was called the SED, the Special Engineer Detachment. Most of them came to Los Alamos and lived in army barracks. I worked with a number of them. It seems almost accidental that I wasn't one of them. Many stayed on after the war, and several continue to live in Los Alamos.

12 Nuclear Physics Research at Columbia University

My experience with neutron interactions with uranium at Princeton introduced me to only a small part of the general field of nuclear reactions. Nuclear physics started with the discovery of radioactivity by Bequerel in 1896. Rutherford began to irradiate targets with alpha particles. His work led him to propose the existence of the atomic nucleus in 1911. Nuclear physicists began to use alpha particles, neutrons, and protons to interact with any elements of interest in the periodic table. Two decades after Rutherford's proposal, the development of particle accelerators made proton bombardment available for the study of the nuclear structure of a variety of targets and eventually led to the discovery of the transmutation of elements and of fission.

Physicists learned to exploit the unique ability of neutrons to probe nuclei. The interactions of neutrons of known energy with various elements demonstrate the existence of resonance scattering and capture at sharply defined energy levels. This kind of research usually begins with the production at a cyclotron of bursts of neutrons of varying energy. The neutrons are separated in energy by time of arrival at the end of an evacuated pipe, the most energetic arriving first and the least energetic last. Their interactions with targets of interest yield enormous amounts of information about the structure and properties of nuclei.

One of the important early uses of the cyclotron at Columbia University was to perform this kind of research. In 1945 our work with plutonium at the Met Lab came to an end. I was told on the telephone by an army colonel to go to Los Alamos. At the same time I was invited by John Dunning, a leader in the program to separate uranium-235 by gaseous diffusion and director of the Columbia nuclear physics program, to join his distinguished group. Although I was concerned that the Los Alamos colonel would intervene, I accepted Professor Dunning's invitation. My task was to obtain and prepare targets of exotic elements for time-of-flight neutron bombardment. It was an invaluable experience for two reasons. I learned how to separate neutrons by energy by time-of-flight. I also had the privilege of working with and being inspired by leading scientists in nuclear physics research, including Madame C. S. Wu and James Rainwater. In later years both received the Nobel Prize. William Havens, later Secretary of the American Physics Society, became a good friend and a trusted source of advice.

On weekends I explored Manhattan on foot from the Bronx to the Battery. Saturday nights were frequently spent at smoky "Nick's" in Greenwich Village. It was the best place to hear the jazz greats of the time. I would drink too much beer, hail a cab back to my room at 93rd and Amsterdam, buy the Sunday *New York Times,* and read it before I went to bed.

Years later, in the 1960s, when I was director of radiochemistry activities at Los Alamos, I used my earlier experience at Columbia in Project Gnome near Carlsbad, New Mexico, and later at the Nevada Test Site, for a unique application of nuclear weapons tests for scientific research. The huge, practically instantaneous burst of neutrons that accompanied the explosion was led down a long, evacuated pipe to a massive shield. A sheet of target material mounted on a rapidly spinning wheel faced a slit in the shield. The moment of explosion was marked on the wheel by activation of the target material within the slit width by the fastest, most energetic neutrons. They arrived almost instantaneously. Neutrons that had been slowed down in a moderating material arrived at distances from the initial slit width that corresponded to their velocity. Strips of the target, each the width of the slit, were highly activated at each neutron capture resonance energy level and registered on X-ray film and could be cut out for chemical analysis. The interaction products were separated and measured at many different resonance capture levels. We exposed wheels of highly enriched uranium-235 to these neutron beams and discovered that the symmetry of fission varied with the value of the spin that was assigned to each resonance level. These experiments provided information about fission that was not obtainable by any other technique. It has since been repeated with various target materials by numbers of teams of nuclear physicists with access to nuclear weapons tests.

LEFT: At age five, I wear a Lord Fauntleroy suit made by my mother. She was a skilled seamstress who used her foot-operated sewing machine almost daily. Sewing napped fabric requires special techniques. She had no problems with it.

BELOW: I am standing next to Mother at age six in the newly acquired family grocery store. I went to work there after school at age nine. Within a few years I became expert at butchering sides of beef, pork, and lamb and grinding large amounts of hamburger.

LEFT: The itinerant photographer provided the Shetland pony. Horses hitched to wagons were still almost as common as automobiles but, until this encounter at age seven, I had never actually sat on a horse or pony. It was a new and thrilling experience.

ABOVE: I met Charles Schon in the fifth grade at the Oxford Street elementary school. He became my closest friend until early years in high school when we discovered girls. They were interested in handsome Charlie.

BOTTOM LEFT: Before posing for my graduation portrait in 1937, I had to earn twenty dollars to buy the new suit I am wearing in this picture. The pants and coat sleeves were generously hemmed to provide for growth. It was my dress-up suit through college.

LEFT: During my freshman year at Worcester Polytechnic Institute, my homework assignments were not very demanding. The difficulty level increased sharply the following year, and I had to spend most evenings working at my home desk.

BELOW LEFT: My draft board in Massachusetts kept classifying me 1-A during the war years, making me subject to immediate entry into the army. My employer would appeal, which had the effect of retaining my civilian status for a few months. Finally, the draft board received a ruling that granted me a deferment by the Office of the President. This was so unusual that they sent me a copy underlining "President" and adding an exclamation point.

ABOVE: A photo of a 1939 LaSalle convertible, the automobile classic in which my longtime friend, newly discharged Air Force captain Irv Lande, drove me from Columbia University in New York to Los Alamos, New Mexico, in late 1945.

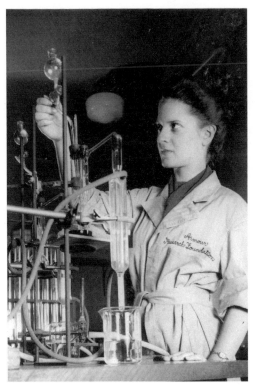

LEFT: I first met Helen Siegel Dunham when I kissed her under a branch of mistletoe at a laboratory Christmas party in 1943. She was my lab partner during her final months at the Met Lab, leaving to go to Los Alamos in the spring of 1945. I arrived there in late 1945 and married her in Santa Fe in 1946. She was a member of the staff at the Armour Research Laboratory in Chicago when this picture was taken in 1943, shortly before she came to the Met Lab.

RIGHT: General Groves, the head of the Manhattan Project, was not popular with most of the Project's scientists. The month before I arrived at Los Alamos, he had come there to preside over a public ceremony in which he awarded citations of merit to the lab and all of its employees. One of the honorees took this picture of the general at the ceremony, and it became almost de rigueur to mount copies of it on every residence wall at Los Alamos.

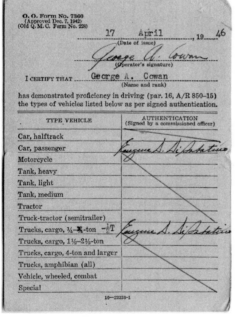

NOTES

1. To be issued only after strict and practical examination.
2. Permit will be authenticated by commissioned officer immediately after test for each type of vehicle concerned.
3. Where testing facilities do not permit cross-country driving, permit will be marked "limited" after each type of vehicle concerned.
4. List accidents below. If more than three are charged to the permit holder, his driving ability and mental attitude should be investigated before issuance of new permit.

RECORD OF ACCIDENTS

(List all in which permit holder is involved)

Date _____ (1)
Responsibility
  and cause _____

Estimated cost of damages _____

_____ Officer's initials _____

Date _____ (2)
Responsibility
  and cause _____

Estimated cost of damages _____

_____ Officer's initials _____

Date _____ (3)
Responsibility
  and cause _____

Estimated cost of damages _____

_____ Officer's initials _____

Passed U. S. E. D. Test

MOTOR VEHICLE OPERATOR'S

Q-1

PERMIT

4278

Valid { with ~~xxxxxx~~ } glasses

MANHATTAN DISTRICT

(OPERATOR'S A. S. N.)

U. S. GOVERNMENT PRINTING OFFICE   16—22236-1

O. O. Form No. 7360
(Approved Dec. 7, 1942)
(Old Q. M. C. Form No. 228)

17   April   , 19 46
(Date of issue)

George A. Cowan
(Operator's signature)

I CERTIFY THAT ____George A. Cowan____
(Name and rank)

has demonstrated proficiency in driving (par. 16, A/R 850–15) the types of vehicles listed below as per signed authentication.

TYPE VEHICLE	AUTHENTICATION (Signed by a commissioned officer)
Car, halftrack	
Car, passenger	Eugene A. DiSabatino
Motorcycle	
Tank, heavy	
Tank, light	
Tank, medium	
Tractor	
Truck-tractor (semitrailer)	
Trucks, cargo, ¼–¾-ton –½T	Eugene A. DiSabatino
Trucks, cargo, 1½–2½-ton	
Trucks, cargo, 4-ton and larger	
Trucks, amphibian (all)	
Vehicle, wheeled, combat	
Special	

16—22236-1

ABOVE AND LEFT: A state driver's license was not accepted for use of official vehicles at Los Alamos. They were mostly military. Operation of one required a driver's training course and a special license. I took the course and received a license for passenger cars and trucks in April 1946.

ABOVE: The original laboratory technical area, TA-1, was built around the site of the Ranch School on South Mesa. These pictures of TA-1 were taken in 1946 and 1947. The area is now part of downtown Los Alamos. (Photographs courtesy Laboratory Archives, Los Alamos National Laboratory)

ABOVE: In 1946 the western fringe of Los Alamos was chosen for expansion of government-built housing for families. It was called the Western Area. This is a predevelopment picture of the Western Area in 1946 showing the original Los Alamos Boy's School horse stables. The home in which we live is located very close to where these stables stood. Stables were moved to the undeveloped eastern end of North Mesa and private ownership of horses grew considerably. (Photograph courtesy Laboratory Archives, Los Alamos National Laboratory)

LEFT: Edward Teller was one of the early scientists at Los Alamos. Like every other employee, he had to wear an identification badge. This war-time photo was attached to his badge. (Photograph courtesy Laboratory Archives, Los Alamos National Laboratory)

ABOVE: We left Los Alamos on September 7, 1946, the day we were married, and went to Carnegie Tech in Pittsburgh. I became a graduate student in physical chemistry and Helen was appointed a research assistant to Dr. John (Jake) Warner, then dean of graduate studies and, later, president of the university. He made it part of my graduate student's education to finish a pitcher of martinis on a visit to his home and remain coherent. He served Beefeater gin.

13 I Go to Los Alamos

Former coworkers, now resident at Los Alamos, called and urged me to come to New Mexico. I agreed and left Columbia University in late 1945. A close friend, a newly discharged fighter pilot still wearing his uniform and medals, picked me up in New York in his resurrected, beautiful 1939 La Salle convertible, and we took off for New Mexico. As we were ready to leave Denver for Santa Fe, I tried to put a call through to Los Alamos. The long-distance operator had no telephone number for Los Alamos. I said, "Try P.O. Box 1663 in Santa Fe." She said with a little edge in her voice, "There are no telephones in P.O. boxes." I said, "Please try." She called Santa Fe and giggled, "I have a gentleman here who wishes to call P.O. Box 1663." The voice at the other end said, "I'll put you through," which she promptly did.

We arrived in Santa Fe and stayed at La Fonda, the town's major hotel. It was Christmas week and the lobby was jammed with people enjoying their first end-of-the war big holiday. A petite, attractive chemist came down from Los Alamos and joined us. She was Helen Dunham, a former colleague at Chicago.

Soon after we had checked into our rooms, people began knocking on our doors. The water mains at Los Alamos had frozen solid, and our visitors were unbathed scientists who wanted to use our showers. We accommodated all requests and sent out for a large supply of fresh towels. Everyone was offered a drink of scarce bourbon from a case that had been sold to us by a patriotic liquor store proprietor in Mexico, Missouri. He said it was a tribute to my Air Force friend's medals. What would now be called heavy drinking and smoking were essential social skills in those days. Our party was almost sedate by local standards. Soon a house detective came to our door to find out what was going on. He was invited to join a rather drunk gaggle of eggheads but only shook his head and left.

Not long after I reported to work at Los Alamos I was asked to join a support group to assist the U.S. Navy in planning and carrying out Operation Crossroads at the Bikini Atoll in the South Pacific. The navy wanted to measure the effect of atomic bombs on various kinds of ships, ranging from destroyers to aircraft carriers and battleships. I was one of about a dozen radiochemists whose job was to measure the actual performance of Trinity-type bombs of nominally 20-kiloton yield. The tests, predictably designated Able, Baker, and Charlie, would include an airdropped bomb and two underwater explosions, one shallow in Bikini harbor and the other in deep ocean. We were to collect airborne debris with remotely controlled aircraft that would fly through the cloud. The underwater explosions would also require the processing of seawater samples collected from the test sites.

I prepared to leave Los Alamos for the Pacific late in May but had made sure that my schedule permitted me to attend the birthday celebration in Los Alamos of an old friend, Wright Langham. We were colleagues at the Met Lab until he joined the early Los Alamos contingent. His party was in full swing when it was interrupted by an urgent phone call. Wright was directed to report to work immediately. Louis Slotin and Al Graves, Los Alamos physicists, had been performing an experiment like one that had gone wrong a few months earlier and killed Harry Daglian, another physicist, with an enormous burst of radiation. The fatal procedure was called "tickling the dragon's tail" and involved assembling the fissionable parts of an atomic bomb to near criticality to make sure that they would do their planned job. They were held slightly apart on the inclined plane of a screwdriver. Something slipped and the assembly went critical.

The next morning several coins in the pockets of Slotin and Graves were delivered to our laboratory. We handled them with tongs. They had been activated by neutron capture and were too dangerous to pick up manually. It was clear that Slotin had received at least as much radiation as had killed Daglian. Graves was standing somewhat behind him and was less exposed but gravely injured. Slotin died several days later. Al recovered in time and fathered children after the accident. He died of a heart attack twenty-three years later. He was director of the Test Division, the home for Los Alamos radiochemists, and was my valued mentor and good friend.

I arrived at Kwajalein in early June 1946 on MATS, the personnel transport arm of the Air Force. Compared to it, today's worst tourist class commercial air travel would be called super deluxe. I wore a prescribed military uniform and had the simulated rank of major. I received salutes from enlisted men but didn't know how to return them. Much of Kwajalein was a miserable third-class military encampment. We were lucky and stayed with a Navy Seebees civilian construction battalion whose members had mostly gone home. It was the only encampment on the island that had hot-water showers. They were officially nonexistent. The bar in the officer's mess served beer for a nickel and whiskey for a dime. The food was excellent, not a word commonly used to describe meals on Kwajalein. The island was inhabited mostly by the Air Force. Navy food standards were considerably higher.

We worked at the airstrip with Air Force personnel. They had modified a number of B-17s that could be flown remotely, commanded by small radios with toggle switches. Skilled operators would send commands to the pitch, roll, yaw, fuel supply, flaps, and brakes of these sampler planes. They were controlled from mother B-17s flying within their sight or by ground-based controllers during takeoffs and landings. The system was new and relatively untried, a common practice with urgent innovations during and immediately after the war.

On the day of the underwater test I joined the crew of a B-17. We took off from Kwajalein Island and assumed control of the drone that had departed under ground control directly behind us. We gained altitude to 16,000 feet and leveled off on the way to Bikini. B-17s were not pressurized and the crew wore oxygen masks above 12,000 feet. As a civilian, I wasn't officially there so I had no mask and simply breathed more deeply through the entire exercise.

An Air Force photographer was on board. He removed the door on the port side of the plane and looked directly toward the zero point. He carefully strapped himself and his equipment to buckles by the side of the door. We were now circling the impressive fleet of navy ships moored in the bay. The drone was off our wing. We were supposed to be at least two miles from the detonation point but our pilot was obviously creeping closer. The voice of the test manager began the last ten-second countdown. At "Zero" the brilliant flash was dimmed by the overlying water, but the entire bay seemed to rise toward us. Then the shock wave arrived. It would have stripped the wings off a plane less sturdy than a B-17. The photographer hadn't practiced this part of the exercise. He and his equipment tumbled through the door and dangled outside on straps. We pulled him and his cameras back in.

Our pilots were now steering the drone into the cloud that obscured the sky ahead of us. It penetrated the cloud and took its samples. We headed back to Kwajalein where I joined my colleagues in retrieving highly radioactive filters from drone samplers. Our photographer's work entered the history books. His picture of the huge "wedding cake" of water and vapor rising from the bay, with ships decorating the cake fringes, has been published countless times.

On my return to Los Alamos, I found a letter from John C. (Jake) Warner, head of the chemistry department at Carnegie Tech. I was accepted for graduate studies, subject to a performance review at the end of my first year. I would be appointed to a teaching assistantship. Norris Bradbury, now assured that Los Alamos would not be dismantled but would become the designated nuclear weapons laboratory of the proposed Atomic Energy Commission, urged staff members to affirm their desire to stay on indefinitely or to resign immediately and receive travel expenses to a new home. I agreed to appear in Pittsburgh in mid-September and then proposed marriage to fellow chemist Helen Dunham (aka Satch). We were married on September 7 in Santa Fe at the home of the local Methodist minister. The best man and best lady were our old friends, Wright and Ruby Langham. A few colleagues attended the ceremony and joined our wedding luncheon at La Fonda. We were serenaded by Billy Palou's wandering minstrels, long-time favorites at the hotel.

Wright and Ruby drove us to the Albuquerque airport. We boarded a TWA flight to Kansas City where we were picked up by my new brother-in-law, Lindley Dunham, and his recent bride. It was nearly dawn when we arrived at the Dunham farm in north-central Missouri, near Macon. We were shown to our bedroom for a long-delayed wedding night and reappeared only in time for a midday big meal celebration and introduction to my bride's family.

I had been warned not to tell her maternal grandfather, a lifelong Republican, that I was a Democrat. The first question Grandpa Lindley asked was, "Young man, what is your political persuasion?" I didn't win him over when I stammered, "Independent." The rest of the immediate family, mother and father, two brothers, and a sister, seemed to be inwardly amused by Helen's choice. I grudgingly abided by a ban on the use of tobacco and alcohol in the house. This rule seemed to have arrived in America when a member of the maternal side of the family joined Penn's colony of Quaker refugees. The code of conduct for the current generation of the Missouri family has since changed. Wine is now quite acceptable.

After a visit at Chicago's Palmer House with friends still working at the Met Lab, we arrived in Worcester in the middle of a record-breaking heat wave. Our reception by my family was polite but had an air of tolerance similar to the Missouri experience. Helen was a *shiksa* from the Wild West. We were both relieved when we eventually got to neutral territory in smoky Pittsburgh.

14 The Pittsburgh Years

During our first several weeks we spent long hours searching for suitable housing. It was hard to find in postwar Pittsburgh. For a while we lived in the attic of an old mansion in Squirrel Hill, near the Carnegie Tech campus. After pursuing a lot of leads, we found a decrepit apartment on North Highland Avenue in East Liberty. We felt lucky. We could escape to Highland Park and watch cardinals and thrushes and pretend we were in a lush countryside, despite the fact that the Pittsburgh smog occasionally became deadly.

Jake Warner offered Helen a job as a lab assistant in his research program. We now had two salaries and felt prosperous. We were pleasantly surprised to discover that we had come to an innovative cultural center. Our extra cash allowed us to go regularly to wonderful Pittsburgh Symphony concerts conducted by Fritz Reiner. The drama school specialized in Shakespeare performed by talented students, many of them going on to successful careers in the theater, TV, and Hollywood.

We constantly played records at home. I had built a little push-pull amplifier in Los Alamos that passed as high-fidelity equipment in those days. We began to acquire an impressive collection of 28-rpm shellacs, followed by 33–1/3 vinyls that introduced us to the exciting new world of LP technology and stereo sound.

On campus, courses and lab work were demanding. My thesis mentor, Paul Fugassi, decided I had skills in the synthesis of exotic compounds and suggested a research topic that required commercially unobtainable tertiary isobutyl formate. I could buy tertiary isobutyl chloride. When combined with silver formate, it would produce a precipitate of highly insoluble silver chloride, leaving behind the desired tertiary butyl formate. However, although silver formate is mentioned briefly in the literature, I could find no evidence that it actually existed or had ever been successfully made. I decided to neutralize silver hydroxide with formic acid in acetone, an organic solvent in which the product, silver formate, would be insoluble and would precipitate.

All went as planned. However, I quickly discovered that silver formate is highly unstable and explodes when dried unless it is handled with extreme care. When I showed some of it to Professor Fugassi, he began to poke at it with a spatula. It exploded with a very loud bang. I had instinctively moved behind him and escaped shards of flying glass. Professor Fugassi was not so fortunate, but his wounds soon healed. I learned to be even more cautious. A fortunate end result was that we obtained a patent for the synthesis of silver formate and sold it to a rocket manufacturer, Aerojet General, for several thousand dollars. Some of the proceeds helped pay my way through graduate school.

15 I Return to Los Alamos

I finished work for my doctorate studies in chemistry at Carnegie Tech and returned to Los Alamos in August 1949 to join the newly formed radiochemistry group. The group leader was Roderick (Rod) Spence, who, like Wright Langham, was a former colleague at the Met Lab. We enjoyed each other's company, and I was delighted to come back to Los Alamos to work under his supervision. Helen returned to her wartime job as an expert on plutonium chemistry. Housing was scarce, but I had asked for a rather nice apartment and, after some initial paper shuffling, moved into much better quarters than we had been able to find in postwar Pittsburgh.

Four weeks after I arrived Rod Spence came into my shiny, new laboratory, carefully closed the door behind him, and asked if I had brought in any radioactive material. I said not yet. He then announced that my lab was being taken over for a special mission and that I would move elsewhere. He offered no further explanation. I wondered about my eviction for a moment and then asked, "Have the Russians done something?" This led to a conversation in which I was added to a small list of people who would work on a sample of radioactive dust that would soon arrive in Los Alamos. No one was to be told about it, including Norris Bradbury, the laboratory director.

For the first time I learned that the Air Force had established a highly secret organization called AFOAT-1, a group of civilians and Air Force officers tasked with the analysis of samples of airborne debris collected by aircraft patrolling along the eastern edges of continental Russia.

Several weather reconnaissance B-29s were specially modified to scoop and filter large volumes of air coming across regions of interest in the Soviet Union. The intent was to monitor and analyze emissions from Russia's expanding nuclear technology. On September 7 a contractor laboratory, Tracerlab West, reported that it had identified radioactive fission products in one of the samples they had received and that the distribution of these products indicated that they had originated in a nuclear explosion. Los Alamos was now being asked to provide backup evidence. Rod Spence sent John Balagna, a former member of the SED at Los Alamos and now a member of the radiochemistry group, to San Francisco on September 10 to pick up a filter sample from Tracerlab.

Various kinds of explosions can disperse a cloud of radioactive debris. A large chemical explosion in a plant processing fuel rods from a nuclear reactor is one possibility. A runaway fission chain reaction in a nuclear pile could be another. A third source, the one of chief interest to U.S. intelligence people, could be the deliberate test of a nuclear weapon. It is possible to demonstrate the exact nature of the source by measuring the ratios of suitable short-lived fission products to long-lived products in the sample. If all the products had been made over an extended period, the longer-lived products would have accumulated and the short-lived products would have largely decayed away. If all the products had been made essentially instantaneously in the explosion of a nuclear weapon, the short-lived products would be at their maximum values compared to the long-lived isotopes. Corrected for the relatively brief delay in collection and analysis, the ratios demonstrated that all the products had been made in one brief moment and fixed that moment quite accurately in time. Thus, we not only knew that the Russians had tested a bomb-like device, but we also had a reasonably accurate estimate of when the test had occurred. Earliest estimates centered on a test date of August 27. We now know that the actual test date was August 29 and that the place was Semipalatinsk in Kazakhstan.

Further analysis of the debris revealed that the Russian device resembled in every respect one of our own weapons, the Trinity device we had tested in southern New Mexico in July 1945, detonated over Japan the following month, and twice used in Operation Crossroads the following year at Bikini. The pattern was familiar and unmistakable. But there were other voices in Washington. A number of people in the intelligence community had predicted that a Russian bomb was several years down the road, that it simply couldn't have been produced by 1949. Therefore, the radiochemistry was faulty and the debris probably originated in a nuclear accident. However, the radiochemical information was redundant and provided the same answer in various ways. A panel of distinguished experts, chaired by Vannevar Bush, a veteran head of federal scientific agencies, was convened in Washington on September 19. The group listened to representatives from Tracerlab, Los Alamos, and other interested parties, and concluded that the Russians had tested a bomb. On September 23, President Truman announced that "within recent weeks an atomic explosion occurred within the U.S.S.R." He was still skeptical and refused to refer to an atomic bomb.

Only weeks later a memorandum began to circulate in Washington that the Russians were so competent and innovative that they might now be well ahead of us in developing a thermonuclear weapon of vastly greater power than the atomic bomb. This new device was frequently referred to as the "Super." This view was presented in detail to President Truman. The author was Edward Teller who argued that Russian reactors might well be moderated with heavy water rather than, as with U.S. reactors, graphite. If so, they would produce excess neutrons that could be absorbed in lithium to make tritium. A thermonuclear device that relied on the reaction between deuterium and hard-to-get tritium would be certain of success. At the end of the year the president resolved the problem by directing Los Alamos to immediately undertake the task of designing and testing a thermonuclear device in the shortest possible time.

16 The Hydrogen Bomb

The laboratory quickly went back to a wartime level of operation, a six-day workweek, extended hours per day, and a feverish program of theoretical analysis and experiments. Edward Teller was now back at Los Alamos, consulting with staff people on every aspect of the new program. Intensive calculations on the classic Super were discouraging. Following a year of intensive effort that failed to produce an acceptable design, Stan Ulam made a promising suggestion to Teller. It involved placing a nuclear bomb in a heavy case and directing the material shock wave to a thermonuclear secondary. Teller modified Stan's suggestion in a way that was quickly recognized as a breakthrough. He proposed to abandon the material shock wave and use radiation from the primary to compress the secondary. Less than two years later Los Alamos conducted "Mike," a design that was based on the Teller version of a two-stage thermonuclear device.

The Mike experimental plan relied on radiochemists to measure the efficiency of thermonuclear fuel burn. The problem was much more difficult than the measurement of the number of fissions in a uranium or plutonium bomb. There are many fission products that can directly characterize the total number of fissions in a sample. The ratio of this number to the amount of fissile material in the sample allows the calculation of the efficiency of the explosion. However, when thermonuclear fuel burns, the end products are only water and helium, too common in the atmosphere to be useful diagnostically. The efficiency of burn had to be measured with suitable target elements, called detectors, inserted in the fuel and activated by fast thermonuclear neutrons. A young graduate student from the University of Chicago, Dick Garwin, had come to Los Alamos and quickly suggested that we develop this technique for use in Mike. Rod Spence asked me to work with Dick in a search for appropriate detectors. The result was an extensive development program that identified a number of detector elements. Several were incorporated into the weapon design.

A later advisor on my new project was Herb York, just finishing his graduate work at Berkeley. Herb wanted to insert detectors in the fuel that would be activated by deuterons. They would serve to measure the temperature of the reacting fuel. I agreed to investigate deuteron reactions on several interesting target elements and eventually coauthored a paper in the *Physical Review* with Herb that summarized our results. An initially puzzling aspect of our relationship was his constant interruptions by telephone calls from Edward Teller. When the formation of a second weapons lab at a failing military project in Livermore, California, was announced in early 1952, with Herb as its director, the subject of all those telephone calls from Edward became clear.

The urgency of the Los Alamos program led to the establishment of a test area in the Nevada desert, only a couple hours' drive from Las Vegas. Tests were first conducted there in 1951. As with the first test in New Mexico, bombs were placed in towers and exploded only when winds blew over unoccupied stretches of desert. Of course, airborne debris eventually passed over inhabited areas, but it was casually assumed that radiation exposures to humans would be small. The rules were much more relaxed then than they are now.

My chief problems were acrophobia and sunburn. We worked several hundred feet above the desert floor standing on swaying platforms of steel or aluminum strip. If I looked down, I turned a light shade of green. I had to learn to look only straight ahead. It was also important to find a shaded spot. The Nevada sun was merciless and temperatures could easily rise into the 100s.

On weekends between tests we escaped to the swimming pools and tables of the handful of casinos on the Las Vegas strip. Except for the slot machines, the smallest bets at the various tables were one dollar, placed with silver dollars or chips. It wasn't uncommon to see people carrying bags that contained several pounds of silver dollars.

The Desert Inn was the fanciest and most popular casino. Las Vegas was beginning to attract large weekend crowds from the West Coast, particularly the Los Angeles area. On Saturday nights there were not enough crap tables to handle the crowds, and would-be gamblers stood three deep at the tables waiting to place bets. When there were many people waiting to play, it became profitable to increase the rate at which gamblers went broke and fresh money came to the table. At such times a beautiful young woman was likely to become the dice thrower, behaving like a novice who had never played the game before. The professional gamblers at the table would whisper to one another and discontinue betting.

The beautiful new dice thrower was more likely to throw a losing two, three, or twelve, so-called craps on her first, or come-out, roll than a winning seven or eleven. One very busy Saturday night I decided to bet that the newcomer would roll many craps and placed my money accordingly. My luck improved and I began to double my bets. About the time I started to feel unusually prosperous, a hefty, unpleasant-looking person showed up at my side and said, "That's enough, Buster." I looked into a pair of steely eyes and took his advice, gathered my chips, and left the casino. The professional gamblers nodded and seemed to understand. I had never heard of Wilbur Clark, Bugsy Siegel, or *The Godfather*, but I was learning the rules in the Las Vegas of the early fifties.

A crucial, modest yield, proof of principle design, named "Greenhouse George," was successfully tested in the Pacific in May 1952. I had placed several pounds of tungsten powder outside the device to be activated by its neutrons. It was the beginning of an expanding program of research involving the production of radioactive isotopes in bomb tests. I traveled to Eniwetok as an observer, accompanied by consultant Anthony (Tony) Turkevich, chemistry professor at the University of Chicago, who had participated in the first test at Trinity Site in July 1945. Greenhouse George was a resounding success.

The Mike device was tested on November 1, 1952. I was aboard the USS *Estes*, the test command ship. I partnered on a small experiment with Fred Reines, who later won a Nobel Prize for detecting and counting neutrinos. We trained a few sailors to help us measure the rate of rise of the bomb cloud. When the bomb went off, the fireball and cloud were so awesome that we all forgot our routines and simply stared. After a while the fireball yield measurement was announced. The initial value was 11 megatons. I better understood our initial sense of disbelief and amazement.

As soon as the yield estimate was available, I boarded a helicopter, transferred to a nearby aircraft carrier, and, seated in back of a navy pilot in the cockpit of a dive-bomber, was catapulted into a flight to Kwajalein. Stuffed into the one-man seat beside me was Herb Grier, a partner in the Edgerton, Germeshausen, and Grier firm that made yield measurements on most of the lab's weapons tests. We suffered in silence until we rolled to a stop in Kwaj. We were greeted on the tarmac by the commanding officer and then transferred to transportation provided by Rod Spence. He was busy recovering filter papers from the returning manned F-84 sampler aircraft. One plane and pilot were missing, presumably having moved too close to the bomb site and blown out of the air by the unexpectedly large yield. The samples were loaded aboard a waiting C-54 and I climbed in after them. We promptly took off, bound for the States via Hickam Field in Honolulu. I was now a courier, bringing back debris samples to Los Alamos.

We landed in Albuquerque in a heavy snowstorm. I was still in light skivvies. Someone helped wrap me in a blanket, and I was driven to Los Alamos in a truck with samples loaded on the back bed. My fellow radiochemists were eagerly waiting to greet me when I reached home. I was the first person back from the test.

17 New Heavy Elements

The debris from Mike contained surprises. The energy produced in the explosion came partly from the fusion burning of deuterium to helium. The fusion process also makes fast neutrons plus protons. Many of the fast neutrons produced fissions in uranium-238, thereby greatly increasing the overall energy yield. However, a majority of the neutrons simply slowed down in the deuterium and were captured in the uranium without producing fission.

The exposure of uranium to slow neutrons was enormously higher than had ever been even remotely possible in previous laboratory experiments. As a result, many uranium nuclei captured large numbers of neutrons successively, an amazing phenomenon with important scientific consequences. When radiochemists analyzed the debris, they quickly found previously unknown plutonium of mass 244, six mass units higher than uranium-238. Processing of larger samples at Berkeley produced a series of heavier isotopes of americium, curium, berkelium, californium, and, finally, two previously undiscovered elements, now known as einsteinium and fermium. The heaviest product identified was fermium-255. Uranium-238 nuclei had captured as many as seventeen neutrons consecutively! The quantities of successively heavier capture products resembled a Poisson distribution. It is the probability distribution, named after the mathematician who first formulated it, when certain kinds of events happen independently and randomly at a given rate over a fixed period of time and affect a target population. An example would be the random mailing of enough letters to the addresses in all the telephone directories in the United States to guarantee that most people would get, say, two letters. The Poisson distribution would give the probability that you would get one, two, three, or several.

Mike was the first time man had ever duplicated something that even faintly resembled what nature has accomplished countless times in the Universe in the explosions of old stars that collapse on themselves and produce unimaginably large bursts of thermonuclear energy and light. Their luminosity decays over a period of months as these supernovae become embers, observable only as huge circles of expanding debris. These explosions produce enormous numbers of consecutive neutron captures that dwarf what was seen in Mike. This phenomenon is called the "r" process, meaning rapid neutron capture, in the description of the synthesis of elements in the Universe by supernovae.

The unexpectedly large flux of neutrons in Mike burned up significant fractions of the radioactive products made in detectors we had placed in the fuel. In addition, the explosion vaporized the atoll and added uranium from the coral to the uranium in the device. The initial radiochemical estimates of yield and efficiency of thermonuclear burn were low and grossly incorrect due to these effects. Early estimates of the Mike yield had to be obtained by movies that measured details in the luminosity and expansion of the fireball.

18 Thermonuclear Testing, 1954–1955

The first stockpile versions of thermonuclear weapons were tested in 1954 at Operation Castle in the Pacific. The Bravo test of the device named "Shrimp" used solid lithium deuteride fuel, enriched in lithium-6 that captured neutrons and made tritium. This hydrogen isotope reacted quickly with deuterium to make a helium atom and another neutron. The test of Shrimp produced a much larger yield than predicted and a heavy fallout pattern of radioactive debris that had a tragic consequence. The nearby presence of a Japanese fishing vessel, the *Lucky Dragon 5*, was not detected and its twenty-three crewmembers received major doses of radiation from the debris. One of the crewmembers died within months of the test, and the others suffered various diseases in later years that were assumed to be related to their exposure.

A new member of the Atomic Energy Commission, Bill Libby, was particularly interested in the contribution of Operation Castle tests to worldwide fallout. I first met Bill in 1948 while visiting Ernie Anderson, my close friend and former colleague at the Met Lab. Bill was Ernie's professor and thesis advisor. Ernie's research problem was to develop low-level counting instrumentation that could measure the amount of radioactive carbon-14 in archaeological samples of plant material taken from ancient Egyptian ruins. He hung an Egyptian amulet on his counter and explained that it increased counting efficiency.

Carbon-14 had been discovered in 1940 by Martin Kamen and Sam Rubin at Berkeley. It decayed to nitrogen-14 with a half-life of 5,730 years. The ratio of carbon-14 to abundant, stable carbon-12 in the archaeological samples was compared with the current ratio to establish the age of the sample and date the ruin. This procedure, called carbon-14 dating, was perfected by Bill, Ernie, and a fellow graduate student, Jim Arnold. The work eventually won the Nobel Prize for Bill Libby.

Shortly after Bill became a commissioner, he asked me to help establish a new initiative, Project Sunshine, dedicated to measuring and minimizing the effect of fallout from weapons tests. He was chiefly concerned with strontium-90, a radioactive fission product with a half-life of 29 years. It behaves like calcium and is absorbed into bone where its radiation might trigger cancer.

Following the Bravo test, I reported the first results from analysis of Shrimp debris to the weapons design group at Los Alamos. We knew nothing of the *Lucky Dragon* incident at the time, but I included an estimate of the amount of strontium-90 produced by Shrimp. When asked about the significance of this number, I said that it was of interest to Bill Libby and his new Project Sunshine. This proved to be true, but it was the shorter-lived fission products that had damaged the *Lucky Dragon* crewmembers. Project Sunshine became an important monitor of the possible long-lived harmful effects of weapons tests.

In August 1953, the Russians exploded "Joe-4," a thermonuclear device heavily fortified with tritium. It was not a weapon but can be characterized as a politically urgent Russian reply to Mike. They called it the "Layer Cake." It was much the same as the Teller "Alarm Clock," the design he had in mind in 1949 when he argued that a tritium-rich design was readily achievable. However, contrary to his suggestion that their production reactors might be moderated with heavy water and could use their excess neutrons to make tritium, the Russians used graphite, just as we did, and, consequently, had no excess neutrons to make the very large quantities of tritium necessary to stockpile the "Layer Cake."

In November 1955, two years later, the Russians tested a "true" thermonuclear device, one that incorporated the Teller-Ulam design using two stages, a fission primary and a thermonuclear secondary inside a heavy case. This was the change that made the Mike design successful. In late 1953 Yuli Khariton, head of the Russian weapon design laboratory, received a rough schematic cartoon of the Teller-Ulam design from Sakharov, the Russian "Teller." It apparently originated from a Russian intelligence source. In addition to the use of a heavy case and the two separate stages, the cartoon contained a puzzling feature. Something, an interstage, had been inserted between the fission primary and the thermonuclear secondary. After a month or two of puzzlement, Khariton realized that the new feature was designed to divert the hydrodynamic shock and that compression of the secondary relied on radiation. Within two months, March and April of 1954, the Russians produced a design concept that was essentially the same as the Mike device. This was the basis for the "Joe-19" device tested in November 1955.

19 Life at Los Alamos in the 1950s

Looking back at those busy and stressful years, I remember sharing a feeling of dedication with my colleagues that equaled our wartime commitment. We were taught to fear Stalin and Russian aggression. The war with North Korea helped feed those fears. We worked long hours but felt deeply rewarded. We were leading the thermonuclear race; the Russians were behind. We were euphoric. The doubts came later.

I was often away from Los Alamos for extended periods. Coming home was always joyful. We usually flew in on Carco, the air taxi service between Los Alamos and Albuquerque. The views of the Sangre de Cristo mountains on the eastern horizon rimming the Rio Grande valley were always breathtaking. On the west side the Jemez Mountains rose to the vast Valle Grande. When I stepped off the plane, I would breathe deeply, partly because the elevation at Los Alamos is over 7,000 feet but also because the thin air had its own delicious aroma.

It was fashionable to complain about the hardships of living in a government town that had retained a considerable part of its drab army camp look. But our house was a compensating feature. It was part of a duplex, built in 1947 when the government decided that Los Alamos would become a permanent facility. It was much more attractive than the third-story apartment we had tolerated in Pittsburgh for three years. It was twelve hundred square feet in area, located on a generous-sized lot with room for flowers and vegetable gardens.

A contract agency, Zia Company, was responsible for providing most of the operational needs of the town and the laboratory. We looked to Zia to fill many daily needs with no charge beyond our low monthly rent. The house was periodically repainted by Zia. Zia fixed the plumbing and leaks in the roof, replaced cracked windows, and sprayed for insects. It also maintained the roads, provided physical security, and ran the school system.

But new employees were likely to have serious complaints. I was made constantly aware of them when I became leader of the radiochemistry group in 1956. There was a perpetual housing shortage. Priorities were assigned according to a point system based on salary and months of residence. Junior employees were placed in jerry-built quadruplex apartments that persuaded many to move off the Hill and commute or simply resign.

I spent a great deal of time dealing with housing problems. The situation improved greatly when we persuaded the AEC to make some of its surrounding land available for purchase by employees. We then learned that Santa Fe and Albuquerque financial institutions were reluctant to finance property in a one-industry town. To solve this problem, some of us formed a savings and loan company and then a national bank that made mortgage loans available to our young people at bargain rates.

An enormous number of Los Alamos organizations promoted various activities, including sports, gardening, star-gazing, production of plays and musical comedies, professional concerts, card games, hiking and mountain climbing, and fine dining. I lost count of the number of houses of worship. Santa Fe helped provide amenities that compensated for Los Alamos minimalism.

In 1958 Helen and I were invited to dinner by Marshall (Marr) and Perrine McCune. Arthur Spiegel and his first bride, residents of Albuquerque, were fellow guests. She was a heavy smoker who died a few years later of lung cancer. The McCunes' home was a gallery for great art. Once seated at the dining room table, I began to stare over Perrine's shoulder at what appeared to be a Rembrandt self-portrait. I had never seen a Rembrandt in a private home. Perrine noticed the attention I was giving the wall behind her. I looked at her questioningly. She nodded and said, "We were very fortunate. My grandmother gave it to us as a wedding present."

Much of our conversation was about the young, struggling Santa Fe Opera that John Crosby had created almost literally out of thin air on the hills of his father's estate just north of Santa Fe. Marr and Perrine were among its major supporters. Helen and I were present at opening night in 1957 and became instant fans and season ticket holders. The Spiegels were also enthusiastic opera lovers. As the evening ended, Marr asked Art and me to join the opera board. We both accepted. It was a truly memorable evening, the beginning of decades of close association with the Opera and of a lifelong friendship with Art and Lib, the high school sweethearts in Chicago who reunited when they both lost their first partners.

John spared no expense in producing summer seasons of opera that aimed at the standards of the world's greatest opera houses. He was not only the artistic director but took on the task of raising millions of dollars per year from wealthy music lovers, many with homes in the Santa Fe area. The early years were a constant struggle. One weekend his debtors were threatening to seize the Opera's assets when it opened its doors on Monday. I had become treasurer of the Santa Fe Opera Foundation and was able, through Los Alamos National Bank, to guarantee a temporary line of credit that solved the immediate problem. Similar crises became a way of life but gradually decreased in number as the support base broadened and the Opera's reputation for excellence helped sell out the house for most performances. Now the Santa Fe Opera is a venerable institution with a sterling international reputation. It is a remarkable tribute to John Crosby's unique talent and dedication.

20 The Nuclear Intelligence Community

Russian intelligence efforts concerning the U.S. nuclear weapons program were quite successful during the Manhattan Project days. The activities of Klaus Fuchs, Julius and Ethel Rosenberg, and numerous other participants in Russian espionage are well documented. It is reasonable to assume that if Russian intelligence in the late 1940s and early 1950s had been equally successful, their weapons designers would have begun to pursue the Teller-Ulam concept in 1951 rather than 1954. Instead, they pursued the Layer Cake, our Alarm Clock, a design too demanding of tritium to stockpile. Their failure to reproduce Mike represents a remarkable three-year hiatus in the efficiency of their espionage apparatus. It is almost axiomatic in the intelligence industry that anything that is known to more than a few people will diffuse and not remain secret to a focused spy network for more than a year or two. I note that if Oppenheimer had been a source of information to the Russians, as was darkly implied later during his clearance hearings, he would surely have promptly disclosed the Teller-Ulam concept.

Much of this kind of information has been collected covertly for many decades but is now expanded and partially declassified by U.S. and foreign laboratories pursuing "nuclear forensics." The term includes the collection, analysis, and attribution of source in the monitoring of possible unfriendly nations or terrorist activities that might involve the use of nuclear materials. Highly sensitive analytical techniques now exist that make it possible to characterize places of interest by the composition of particle samples taken at their locations. New York City particles, for instance, have a signature different from Chicago particles or Moscow particles.

In the early 1950s AFOAT-1, the intelligence community's practitioner of much of early nuclear forensics, established a panel chaired by Hans Bethe that reviewed evidence provided by analyses of a variety of samples associated with known or suspected Russian nuclear activities. The panel also received information gathered by seismic and acoustic monitors. Named after its chairman, the Bethe Panel held regular meetings in Washington and presented its findings in summary sessions that were faithfully attended by representatives of JAEIC, the Joint Atomic Energy Intelligence Committee. The Bethe Panel remained active for more than two decades.

The Washington intelligence community is enormous. Our interactions with an alphabet soup of other sources of information were limited. There were categories for people sources (HUMINT), foreign wireless transmissions (ELINT), and transmissions from various airborne and highly classified satellites. Cryptology (COMINT) was in a category of its own. It was consolidated under the National Security Agency (NSA) in the early 1950s and created a large, gated community at Fort Meade.

A majority of the Bethe Panel members came from the Los Alamos and Livermore laboratories. The Los Alamos members were Carson Mark, Rod Spence, and myself. At various times the group included Edward Teller, Herb York, and Harold Brown. From time to time data obtained from debris samples were inconclusive and invited broad speculation concerning the nature of the test. In such cases the California contingent almost invariably proposed an advanced, highly imaginative design. The Los Alamos people tended to be conservative. Bethe favored conservatism. I recall a session in which Livermore people proposed an interpretation that resembled one of their own untested concepts. Bethe said, "It's time to write our summary. It can be a long document about what we don't know or a short one about what we know." We wrote a short one. He had a unique talent for resolving differences and was the principal reason why Bethe Panel reports were widely accepted by a frequently skeptical intelligence community.

21 The Oppenheimer Hearings

Although Oppenheimer was no longer director of the laboratory, he remained very popular at Los Alamos. His sympathy in the prewar years for Communist Party causes was well known, but his wartime service to his country demonstrated his ultimate allegiance and protected him against repeated attacks by those who distrusted his views.

The Joe-1 test led to our crash effort to make the "Super." Oppenheimer's reservations about the program, particularly concerning its military usefulness, inflamed his critics. In 1953 Lewis Strauss, a major advocate of the Super program, was promoted from a member of the Atomic Energy Commission to its chairman and quickly began to orchestrate a campaign to destroy Oppenheimer's reputation. It led to withdrawal of his clearance followed by hearings before a specially appointed tribunal to decide whether to endorse what was essentially a one-man decision.

I was the corresponding secretary of the Los Alamos chapter of the Federation of Atomic Scientists during the hearings and spent considerable time writing letters to leading journalists asking them to review the charges and come to Oppie's defense. We had some success, but Edward R. Murrow, the most influential television journalist of that time, replied that he had a full agenda. To the best of my knowledge, he paid no further attention to the hearings.

When Lewis Strauss visited Los Alamos, partly at our urging, a small group of Federation members met with him and strongly defended Oppie. Strauss became highly complimentary. He praised us for our interest in this important matter and invited us all to visit with him whenever we came to Washington and to stay at his apartment. We were charmed, shook hands, and left, convinced that things would go better in Washington. We were wrong.

Not long after Oppie lost his clearance, Teller came to Los Alamos. Most of his old associates refused to meet or talk with him. John Manley was vehemently anti-Teller. However, he identified me as a more neutral figure and asked me to meet with Teller in a public debate at Fuller Lodge. Teller wanted to show some evidence of public acceptance at Los Alamos. After a short discussion with Teller, we agreed to avoid the Oppenheimer issue. I suggested a topic, "The Illusion of Power." I argued that in much of history the perception of power was more important than the reality. Now we must focus on promoting the illusion. Actual military use would be truly catastrophic.

The Russians were fully aware of the uses of illusion. The huge brass cannon on the grounds of the Kremlin was never fired but simply shown to visitors who went away awed. It was never meant to be fired. Teller argued that we couldn't depend on illusions, that our power had to be real and superior and demonstrably ready to use. There was a full audience and considerable discussion afterward but no vote. We continued a lively conversation when the audience dispersed. Edward truly believed in the importance of coercive military power. I strongly questioned his views but, in meetings over many years, my respect for Edward's eloquence, passion, and precise use of English remained high.

22 Los Alamos Becomes Privately Owned

In 1954 the AEC asked for legislation from Congress to provide for the disposition of the communities of Oak Ridge and Richland. Richland became incorporated in 1958 as a first-class city, governed by a city manager and a city council, and Oak Ridge followed suit a year later.

In 1962 the AEC asked Congress to amend the enabling legislation to provide for the disposition of Los Alamos. Transfer of municipal functions to Los Alamos County required two charter referenda before it was completed in 1968. Los Alamos chose a form of government similar to that at Oak Ridge and Richland except that it was a combined city-county.

Citizen subcommittees were formed to deal with the AEC and to set up management structures for each of the multitude of functions performed by city governments. They included housing, utilities, businesses, schools, and a large variety of other public and special services. All of the subcommittees were monitored by a central County Planning Committee.

The housing subcommittee had to consider ways to deal with a chronic severe shortage of houses, building lots, and mortgage financing. The only bank in Los Alamos was a branch of the First National Bank of Santa Fe. It was reluctant to invest in Los Alamos mortgages. The scarcity of capital led to formation of two local financial institutions, the Los Alamos Building and Loan Association and the Los Alamos National Bank. They provided much of the funding required for construction of privately owned homes on land purchased from the government on adjacent Barranca Mesa to the north and the nearby suburbs of White Rock and Pajarito Acres along the Rio Grande to the east.

The most contentious transfer involved ownership of the electric and gas utilities. Although telephone service was by far the most profitable, the AEC made it clear at the outset that the system would be transferred to AT&T. The AEC also assumed that gas and electricity would go to the neighboring utilities providers. I chaired a study group that concluded county ownership of utilities was feasible and would provide an important source of revenue. The public was asked to vote on the issue. A heated campaign preceded the election, with extensive radio and press advertising in favor of private ownership funded by Public Service Company of New Mexico and Southern Union Gas Company, the existing area utility providers. The vote was heavily in favor of county ownership.

Once a decision was reached to permit the county to acquire gas, electric, and water utilities, a group was formed to draft a management plan. Drawing on the experience of many other municipally owned utility systems, we drafted a proposal to the county to form a Department of Utilities that reported to an independent board. A number of municipally owned systems suffered from commingling of their revenues with other funds. Safeguards were put in place to ensure that this didn't happen in Los Alamos while providing a formula for transferring net profits to the existing county management. The solution was not universally popular at the time but has proved effective and significantly supportive of the county's fiscal needs.

23 Banking at Los Alamos

The chronic housing shortage and the reluctance of out-of-town banks to provide mortgages for privately built houses in Los Alamos made it increasingly urgent to find fresh sources of money. James (Jimmy) Teare, former manager of the Los Alamos branch of the First National Bank of Santa Fe, organized a small group of investors, including me, to offer loans to local homebuilders. Although my initial motivation was to help provide financing for the promising young people I was attempting to recruit into my laboratory group, I quickly discovered that we had made a profitable business decision. Our organization, the Los Alamos Building and Loan Association, was highly successful. My new employees were happily moving into privately owned homes more splendid than our own government-built house. We were beginning to find an effective mix of government largesse and private enterprise.

I was receptive when Jimmy Teare suggested that we form a community bank. Once again a board of local investors was organized, largely consisting of laboratory people with a sprinkling of representatives from the small business community. We applied for a charter as a national bank. A group of examiners visited us and denied the request on the grounds that the group had insufficient banking experience. We appealed to our representatives in Congress and received their support. A second visit from examiners followed and our request was granted.

The members of the board were each allotted a number of shares. The initial capitalization was set at two million dollars. Founding directors could buy the shares themselves or resell them to other Los Alamos people. My phone began to ring incessantly with would-be investors, and I resold almost all of my allotment. The bank opened its doors in 1963 and, after an initial break-in period, became profitable in 1964. Our chairman of the board, my laboratory division leader Al Graves, died of a heart attack in 1965 and I was named to succeed him. I remained chairman for thirty years. During the bank's early years I bought most of the stock put up for sale by initial investors and became the majority stockholder. Eventually the bank became the largest non-publicly traded bank in New Mexico. It expanded into Santa Fe in recent years and soon became the city's major bank. Its assets were essential to solving the Los Alamos perennial housing shortage.

24 Poker and Theoretical Physics

Card games were a popular social pastime in Los Alamos. In the late 1940s a number of theoretical physicists started to meet regularly to play poker. Carson Mark, head of the theoretical physics group, presided over the table. The group included Stan Ulam, destined to be a nuclear weapon design partner with Edward Teller; Nick Metropolis, the author most cited in science journals by users of his Monte Carlo algorithm for repeated sampling of random numbers in complicated calculations on new electronic computers; Foster Evans, the widely consulted authority on ingenious use of developing computer technology to perform "impossible" calculations; Roger Lazarus, in charge of specifying and acquiring the latest in bigger and better computers; Paul Stein, the authority on number theory and collaborator with Metropolis on Monte Carlo techniques; Jim Tuck, the meticulous Brit who directed research on controlled thermonuclear energy; and Rod Spence, the director of radiochemistry. I happily accepted an invitation to join this interesting group.

The game had less to do with good poker than with conversation, food, and drink. The stakes were low. The chips were worth a dime, a quarter, and a dollar. Carson kept the cards, the chips, the green felt cloth that covered the table, and the accounts that were meticulously settled to the dime at the end of each session. The list of invited guests was long and frequently distinguished. Edward Teller mentions the game in his *Memoirs* (page 302). I particularly liked to see him because he had a tendency to draw to inside straights.

Hosts would take their duties seriously. Stan wanted his coffee fiercely black. Paul loved sardine sandwiches. Nick was fond of exotic Greek olives. Jim insisted on beer at room temperature. Roger liked kosher dill pickles. Carson and Rod were omnivorous but sometimes overlooked the cold beer and asked for Scotch whiskey or bourbon. I usually prepared a corned beef brisket, sliced thin and served with specially ordered dark rye bread.

My wife hated the nights it was my turn to host the game. I suspect that most spouses felt the same way. Smoking was still a universal habit and included cigarettes, cigars, and pipes. Sometimes the smoke obscured the cards. The windows and doors were left open for two or three days after a game. Looking back, I remember only that I enjoyed the true "atmosphere," meaning the friendship and joking. I had given up smoking and breathed shallowly on poker nights.

In sharp contrast, the Los Alamos atmosphere had a pristine quality that I found unique and especially relished when I returned from a trip to anywhere else. My opinion wasn't universally shared. We occasionally went to the Santa Fe home of Ina Sizer Cassidy, a vigorous nonagenerian, widow of the artist Gerald Cassidy whose work is hung on many of the walls at Santa Fe's La Fonda. When we left her compound on Canyon Road to have dinner at a neighboring restaurant, she would extend her upturned palm and say, "The fallout is heavy tonight."

25 Project Gnome: The Add-on Wheel Experiment

Starting in 1958 Russia and the United States honored a moratorium on nuclear weapons tests. It continued until the Russians resumed testing in August 1961. During the moratorium Los Alamos scientists turned their attention to development of nuclear-powered rockets. Many feared that Russia was developing ICBMs (intercontinental ballistic missiles) and doubted chemical fuels could provide enough energy to propel useful payloads over thousands of miles. The Los Alamos program made impressive progress toward developing a nuclear engine, but the program lost its funding when chemical fuels were produced that could do the job.

I used the testing hiatus to organize and chair a conference at Los Alamos on the "Scientific Applications of Nuclear Explosions" and authored a report of the proceedings that was published in a June 1961 issue of *Science*. One of my interests was in using them as neutron sources for time-of-flight neutron spectroscopy measurements, somewhat similar to the work of Dunning's group at Columbia. Teller had established a major program at Livermore, called Project Plowshare, to explore the peaceful uses of nuclear explosions. The first event in this program was the "Gnome" test, deep in a salt mine outside Carlsbad. Its objectives included an exploration of the feasibility of recovering the energy stored in molten salt to drive steam turbines and make electricity and, in addition, to mine the debris for useful radioisotopes.

With the permission of Los Alamos and Livermore, I planned to introduce the first time-of-flight neutron spectroscopy experiment with a nuclear explosion as the neutron source. The Los Alamos Test Division set up a small adjunct office in Carlsbad to carry it out. I traveled to Carlsbad as needed to help in the preparation. Getting there proved to be a pleasant part of the job. I was allowed to fly my Cessna-172 from Los Alamos to Carlsbad since there were no convenient commercial flights. The weather was generally warm and sunny. Crossing New Mexico by air from north to south and back was always a fun experience.

I became concerned about the conditions we would face when we had to recover the wheel. We needed to get it back to Los Alamos as quickly as possible in order to do the necessary chemistry before the fission products of interest decayed to low levels. My team had to go 1,000 feet down the shaft, move through the tunnel to the wheel recovery cable, and bring the wheel back up. I couldn't depend on weather conditions to fly and proposed to drive it back.

When I inspected the tunnel walls, said to be composed of solid sodium chloride, I observed that there were horizontal faults every few feet full of water saturated in salt. I wondered how the formation would stand up to a 3-kiloton blast. Unlike a theoretically uniform granite formation, the salt formation was already riddled with lubricated joints.

It was December 10, 1961. Edward Teller had come to Carlsbad to observe the test. I was standing next to him in the control room as the countdown proceeded. Having played poker with him, I knew he wasn't averse to a bet. I said, "It's going to vent. Bet one dollar." He replied, "I think not. One dollar. All right." Moments after the shot, we felt the rumble. Then, suddenly, steam rose from the shaft. Venting of debris began minutes later at spots along the line of the tunnel. Edward reached for his wallet and handed me a one-dollar bill. I was now busy planning a delayed recovery operation.

Due to persistent high radiation levels, it was six days before we could reenter the tunnel and pull back the wheel. It reached the top of the shaft about 4 AM on the seventh day. There was no one present except my recovery team and the radiation monitoring team. The usual security people were exhausted and off napping somewhere. I drove my station wagon to the shaft head, had the wheel wrapped and dumped in back, and took off for Los Alamos. I stopped at the security gate that led into the test area and was nodded through by the guard.

I had been up for nearly twenty-four hours and now had a 325-mile drive to Los Alamos. The road was dark and lonely. I kept slapping my cheeks and singing loudly but occasionally nodded and moved to the shoulder of the road. Fortunately, in the flat desert I was driving through, there was little difference between the road and the terrain. Then as I turned west to cross the Sandia Mountains and north again to Los Alamos, the road became more challenging and I had no trouble staying awake. The radiochemistry group was waiting when I arrived in full daylight. The delay had lowered our expectations of success. The statistics eventually proved to be inadequate to clearly demonstrate the dependence of the symmetry of fission on the spin values at different resonances in the neutron absorption cross sections. It took several more such experiments over a period of years to definitively demonstrate this kind of spin dependence.

Three months later I had turned to other matters when the wheel experiment suddenly came to life again. Two men had arrived at Los Alamos from Carlsbad. The officials in charge of that site had completed an inventory of accountable materials and discovered that they were missing several kilograms of weapons-grade uranium-235. It had been stolen! After some intensive detective work, they identified the thief and came to Los Alamos to recover the uranium and arrest me. It took a lot of conversation with Norris Bradbury, the laboratory director, and Al Graves, division leader, to convince them to leave without me. The argument that helped send them away was that if the incident came to light, it would probably trigger a congressional investigation and reveal a major fault in AEC security. Despite tighter security at the Nevada Test Site, the whole system would be called into question. The Carlsbad people were given every last gram of uranium, some of it in solution and most of it still in metal form, and I was unofficially reprimanded. The event then became a nonevent.

Edward Teller continued to promote the use of nuclear explosions for peaceful purposes (PNEs), principally to construct coastal harbors where none existed. The program never developed strong support in Washington, partly because of fears about generating radioactive debris in areas that would become open for some practical use and partly because the economic advantages were never fully spelled out. Twenty-eight tests were conducted between 1961 and 1973, none of them leading to a practical application. Funding for Project Plowshare ended in 1977.

The Russians were considerably more active in the use of PNEs. They conducted 239 nuclear tests between 1965 and 1988, six of them described as practical applications. Their program has never been officially terminated but remains dormant and forgotten.

On October 30, 1961, the Russians fired a 50 megaton bomb. The event was publicly announced in advance. The design was readily scalable to 100 megaton. The Russians never said whether it was meant to destroy enemy targets or used to excavate harbors. It had no apparent military purpose. Khrushchev probably directed Sakharov and his weapons designers to produce a modern version of the Kremlin brass cannon.

26 Duplicating Mike Neutron Exposure

Once it became clear that the synthesis in Mike of new elements could be repeated with specially designed, relatively small yield devices, our designers proposed add-ons to scheduled weapons tests that might make even heavier products than had been found in Mike. The add-ons were designed to maximize the neutron density within a relatively small volume of burning thermonuclear fuel surrounding a uranium target and to slow the disassembly time. Following Mike, a number of Los Alamos and Livermore tests included high neutron exposure add-ons. Teller strongly encouraged experiments of this kind at Livermore and they tested a series of add-ons that achieved increasingly large neutron exposures.

Livermore conducted the "Hutch" experiment in July 1969. It made more fermium isotopes than in any previous attempt. However, no new elements were recovered. Seaborg had speculated that an element with 114 protons in its nucleus would be much more long-lived than its neighbors. It would have reached an "island of stability" due to a particularly favorable "magic" configuration of protons at the number 114. If this island existed, it was also possible that elements approaching the island with, say, 110, 111, 112, and 113 protons, would become increasingly stable. The speculations were tested with "Hutch" because it should have made elements much heavier than fermium. However, nothing more long-lived than the alpha-emitter fermium-257 with a 100-day half-life has been made by neutron exposure in an explosive device. To date, all heavier products made in this way are too short-lived to recover from bomb debris.

27 U.S.–U.K. Joint Working Group for Radiochemistry

In 1958 the United States and the United Kingdom entered into a Mutual Defense Agreement (MDA) that reestablished close cooperation between the two countries in efforts related to nuclear weapons development and intelligence. The British equivalent of Los Alamos was the Aldermaston Weapons Establishment, about 12 miles distant from Reading. Dr. Frank Morgan was the person in charge of a division at Aldermaston with broad responsibilities in the processing, fabrication, and analysis of nuclear materials.

Morgan and I became colleagues when, under terms of the MDA, we were appointed co-chairmen of the Joint Working Group for Radiochemistry. It was called JOWOG-20, a number that distinguished it from other JOWOGs. It sponsored meetings and exchanges of information between the laboratories concerning weapons testing and fabrication. Another channel was opened between AFTAC in Washington and Frank Morgan and his associates at Aldermaston for exchange of intelligence concerning weapons tests by other nations, principally the Soviet Union. I was a member of the AFTAC group and met with him under both lab and intelligence auspices. These activities required the frequent exchange of visits to Los Alamos, Aldermaston, Washington, and the Ministry of Defence in London.

Our relationship became a close friendship. He had a dry sense of humor and was a great conversationalist. During my first visit to Aldermaston, I was invited to dinner at his home and learned with great pleasure that his carefully chosen clarets included some of my favorites from the Pauillac and St. Julien regions. His wife was a gracious hostess who had a remarkable assistant, her ten-year-old daughter. Young Janet joined the dinner group and immediately started to draw everybody out, making sure that each of us had equal time. It was a stellar performance. The little girl made the dinner party sparkle.

The Morgans liked to summer in the south of France. We joined them at their rented villas on two of their holidays and filled ourselves with duck, foie gras, ripe figs, fresh trout, and local wines. Frank and Janet liked to talk with neighboring farmers and helped me join in, gently correcting my unschooled accent. All of my visits with the Morgans were pleasurable learning experiences.

My collaborations with Frank continued over many years until his sudden death from a heart attack in April 1985. We had been working on a history of some of our classified joint activities that he felt might become public in time, perhaps after his death. The unfinished work was locked up somewhere at the U.K. Embassy in Washington. Janet knew it existed and encouraged me to locate it some years later. I had no luck.

Janet has provided me with a copy of *Spying on the Nuclear Bear*, by Michael S. Goodman, published in late 2007 by Stanford University Press. It describes a part of Frank's role in surveillance of Russia's nuclear weapons programs. I hope that Janet will eventually write a more comprehensive account of Frank's career at Aldermaston. She has authored a number of biographies, including a definitive, family-authorized work on the life of Agatha Christie. Her remarkable history, *The Secrets of Rue St. Roch*, dealt with the work of the intelligence office that her father-in-law, Lord Balfour of Burleigh, ran in Paris during World War I. She had the help of papers stored for decades in the attic of the ancestral Balfour home in Scotland.

28 International Symposium, Heavy Ion Physics, Dubna, Russia

Particle accelerators were first developed to help explore nuclear physics. They became indispensable military instruments with the discovery of fission in 1938 and, less than three years later, in the production of plutonium at Berkeley. Glenn Seaborg, Art Wahl, and Joe Kennedy first made and then chemically identified plutonium-238 by bombardment of uranium with deuterons in late 1940. In the spring of 1941 they again used deuterons to make neutrons that were captured in uranium-238. They were able to synthesize an identifiable amount of plutonium-239 and demonstrate that it was very fissionable. It was this discovery that suddenly promoted the construction of the uranium chain reactor to a top priority at Chicago. By the end of the war, a new question arose. Could heavy ion accelerators point the way to an island of stability populated by yet-to-be-discovered highly fissionable transplutonium elements? The mere prospect was sufficient to add urgency to their development. Oak Ridge became the center of postwar research with heavy ion bombardments, first with a modified cyclotron and later with the development of the heavy ion linear accelerator (HILAC).

Berkeley got its first HILAC in 1957 and became the new leader in heavy ion bombardment research. Seaborg and Al Ghiorso used it to produce element 102, nobelium, in 1958. In 1957 Georgy N. Flerov established a major facility at the Dubna site of the Joint Institute for Nuclear Research and was soon both a collaborator and competitor with Berkeley in the production of transuranic elements by heavy ion bombardment. In the fall of 1966 Flerov sponsored an international meeting to review progress in this field. It was attended by the rapidly growing international community of researchers who were now working with heavy ion accelerators.

I went to the meeting to report on the achievements and limitations of multiple neutron capture for the production of transuranics. My trip to Russia was interrupted when my Aeroflot flight out of Paris landed in Warsaw, and I was deliberately directed to a group of disembarking passengers. By the time it became apparent to me that I had been misdirected, my plane had departed for Moscow and I was told that I would have to spend the night in Warsaw. My luggage was gone. When I caught up with it the next day in Moscow, my locked bag had been forcibly opened and tied back up with a length of cord. There was no attempt to conceal the search. I had my notebook in a hand-carried briefcase and had brought nothing that I considered sensitive.

I was driven from Moscow to Dubna in a bone-rattling bus and deposited at a hotel on the banks of the Volga. The guests were all from the United States and Western Europe. I was greeted by a Russian friend and given a familiarization tour around town. He pointed out two other hotels, one for visiting Russians and another for visitors from neighboring Communist countries. He said that the second hotel was also in charge of foreign affairs. When I asked him to elaborate, he said that many of the employees were very attractive women. This was not the case at my hotel.

I found an invitation to dinner that evening with Flerov. It was my first meeting with him. He was a genial host. I joined a distinguished group of guests with a heavy representation of people I knew from Berkeley. The conversation was lively, helped by many toasts with a super-abundant flow of vodka. Flerov was quite proud of his wine collection, all from Russian winemakers. It was an opportunity to sample the best regional wines. They didn't suit my Bordeaux- and Burgundy-biased tastes but gave me an appreciation of the regional styles. Solid food came late. I was hungry and stuffed myself on smoked salmon, caviar, pickled herring, chicken Kiev, and dark rye bread slathered with sweet butter.

The next day I left my room early to walk to the conference hall and discovered that I had inadvertently left my notebook in my room.

I turned and went back. The notebook was gone. I spoke to the loud-speaker on the wall, "I'll be gone for ten minutes and will expect to find my notebook." I walked down toward the Volga and returned in ten minutes. My notebook was lying where I had left it on the desk.

On another evening I joined K. A. Petrzhak after dinner at the bar attached to the hotel dining room. Petrzhak was the coauthor with Flerov of a famous 1941 paper announcing the discovery of spontaneous fission in uranium-238. He was now working as an assistant to Flerov in Dubna. He was about my age and a charming conversationalist. Over vodka we began to exchange personal histories. I told him about my work at Princeton in 1941. He told me that he had gone into the Russian army about that time. In February 1943, he was stationed on the front line facing advancing German forces. Casualties were high. He was told to move out to a foxhole and become an artillery spotter. He knew that the average life of a spotter was a few days and began to write farewell letters. He was serving as a spotter when he was told to report urgently to the command bunker. There he was instructed to travel to Moscow and report for a new assignment. When he arrived at the newly organized Kurchatov Institute in Moscow, he was greeted by his former colleague Flerov and his new boss, Igor Kurchatov. They had assembled over a dozen distinguished scientists and were forming a nuclear research laboratory to provide blueprints for a Russian "Manhattan Project." Despite the threat posed by the advancing Germans, the program had a top priority for whatever was immediately needed.

Stalin was obviously responding to intelligence reports about the rapidly expanding Manhattan Project. It is reasonable to assume that his sources had informed him that the Fermi reactor had achieved criticality on December 2, 1942. This news demanded immediate action. Kurchatov and his people would use additional intelligence to plan duplicate designs of the Hanford plutonium production pile and of the Fat Man (the plutonium-core, implosion design) bomb. However, defeat of the Germans had first priority, and construction of a reactor did not get fully under way until the end of the war in August 1945. The production reactor went critical in December 1946, and the first bomb was tested in August 1949. Stalin was surely aware of the circulation in Washington of a proposal for a preemptive attack on Russia before they could achieve nuclear capability. The 1949 test of Joe-1 must have been given an overriding priority. It came considerably earlier than the U.S. and U.K. intelligence communities had predicted.

On our last evening at Dubna I had dinner at the home of a senior researcher followed by a going-away party at our hotel. By 1 AM everyone had toasted everyone else, and most of the visitors had gone off to bed. Many of the Russians were still partying. I said good night and went to my room. As I prepared for bed, someone knocked at my door. I opened it and found my dinner hostess, the wife of the research professor. She had been doing her part in the vodka toasting ceremonies and tilted noticeably to one side. I asked her to come in. As soon as I shut the door she said, "You must help us get out of here." I promised to do whatever I could and then said, "Let me take you back to your apartment." As we walked I looked back and saw a figure dodging from tree to tree. I assumed that it was her husband. Eventually they attended a meeting in Copenhagen and were taken in by a friendly university.

The meeting at Dubna underlined Russia's early leadership in developing the use of heavy ions to make new heavy elements. It has retained and strengthened its position in this field. All efforts to make new elements now rely solely on heavy ion bombardments at particle accelerators. Although an island of stability is still predicted around the doubly magic, exceptionally stable configuration of 114 protons and 184 neutrons (total mass of 298), most predictions now estimate that the longest half-lives will be only hours. Recent experiments have focused on the region of 114 to 118 protons, using heavy actinide targets and stable, very neutron-rich calcium-48 projectiles. Production of element 118 with a half-life of about a millisecond has been reported in bombardments of californium-249 with calcium-48, presumably producing element 118 with 176 neutrons with a total mass of 294 following escape of three neutrons from the compound nucleus. This result will be extremely difficult to verify because it does not decay to a known isotope. To date there have been no reports of heavy nuclei with more than 176 neutrons. It now seems highly unlikely that nature made any elements in this mass region that would exist in our planetary system today. At best, they might exist briefly in the expanding debris of a supernova.

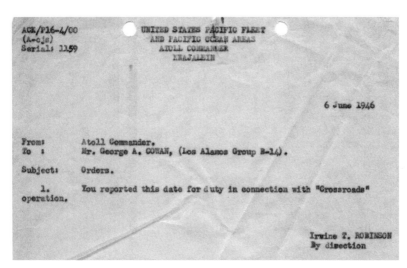

ACK/P16-4/00
(A-cjs)
Serial: 1159

UNITED STATES PACIFIC FLEET
AND PACIFIC OCEAN AREAS
ATOLL COMMANDER
KWAJALEIN

6 June 1946

From: Atoll Commander.
To :   Mr. George A. COWAN, (Los Alamos Group B-14).

Subject: Orders.

1.   You reported this date for duty in connection with "Crossroads"
operation.

Irwine T. ROBINSON
By direction

ABOVE: I reported on June 6, 1946, to the Air Force commander of Kwajalein Atoll for duty with the Operation Crossroads contingent. I was given the simulated rank of major and chose to live in the Seebees encampment because it had hot showers (officially illegal) and the best officers' mess.

ABOVE: Some of my dozen radiochemist colleagues at the Seebee Officers' Club. I am standing on the left. Joe Khym, the card player in the white tee-shirt, was our unofficial supply officer. He provided us with a Jeep, taken from the parking area at the Officers' Club and bearing a repainted number.

SGT. YEHUDI and the BABES

Four robot Fortresses, vanguard of a coming era of pilotless aircraft, are being readied for Operation Crossroads and a flight through the atom cloud

By CHARLOTTE KNIGHT   Air Force Staff

ABOVE: The Air Force had modified a number of B-17 bombers to serve as unmanned samplers of debris from the highly radioactive clouds produced by nuclear explosions. They nicknamed the designer "Sgt. Yehudi," and the sampling drones were called "Babes."

LEFT: This is a picture of a drone landing at the Kwajalein airstrip. The landings were always exciting because controlling the speed and orientation on final approach was an inexact art. As we watched one landing from a jeep next to the runway, the drone veered and came straight at us. We set a new Jeep record for acceleration in reverse.

LEFT: Members of the Air Force sampling contingent listening to radio reports of the progress of the debris sampling operation following the Test Able explosion. The bomb-carrying plane practiced precision drops diligently in the days prior to the test but on shot day missed the target ship, the battleship USS *Nevada*, by about a quarter of a mile.

LEFT: A picture of the rising bubble from the underwater test of Shot Baker in the Bikini harbor. Over ninety expendable navy vessels of various types were anchored around Ground Zero. I was aboard the B-17 mother plane from which this photo was taken. It was guiding a drone sampler. Moments later the plane flew through the bomb-generated shock wave of plus 9 and minus 11 G.

ABOVE: This picture of the Test Baker bomb cloud was taken a few seconds after detonation. The upper umbrella was the region penetrated by drone samplers to capture samples of debris for radiochemical measurements of the energy yield.

TASK GROUP 7.1 KEY PERSONNEL

COWAN, George A.

DATE OF EMPLOYMENT: 1949

DEGREES: D. Sc., Chemistry

SCHOOLS: Worchester Polytechnic
Institute
Carnegie Institute of
Technology

EXPERIENCE: Met Lab, University of
Chicago, 1942-45; LASL,
1945-46; Carnegie Tech,
1946-49

Number of
Operations: 4

Present Position:

Program 11
Leader (J-11,
LASL)

LASL

TASK GROUP 7.1 KEY PERSONNEL

GRAVES, Alvin C.   Nickname: "Al"

DATE OF EMPLOYMENT: April 1943

DEGREES: B. S., Electrical
Engineering
Ph. D., Physics

SCHOOLS: University of Virginia
Massachusetts Institute
of Technology
University of Chicago

EXPERIENCE: Instructor, Univ. of
Texas; Associate Professor 1942-

Number of
Operations: 12

Present Position:

Deputy Commander
for Scientific
Matters

JTF-7, LASL

ABOVE: Excerpts of entries for George Cowan and test director Al Graves from the Operation Castle handbook, 1956. I worked for Al Graves for a number of years. He survived the nuclear criticality accident that killed his colleague, Louis Slotin, in May 1946 but appeared to age more rapidly than normal and died of a heart attack at age 54.

ABOVE: A session of the T-Division (Theoretical Physics Division) poker game with Stan Ulam gathering in chips. The leader of the group was Carson Mark, director of T-Division. It met regularly for a number of years and was known for the number of distinguished scientists who joined the game over the years.

LEFT: Project Gnome was the first test in the Plowshare program, designed to use the 3 kilotons of energy produced in the blast for peaceful purposes. It was exploded in a potash deposit near Carlsbad, New Mexico. It vented and produced high levels of radioactivity along Highway 128 east of Carlsbad. (Photograph courtesy Laboratory Archives, Los Alamos National Laboratory)

LEFT AND BELOW LEFT: The Gnome cavity was reentered in May 1962. Radiation levels had dropped enough to permit short trips to the explosion site. The exposure of potash to intense radiation produced bands of blue, green, and violet salt. (Photographs courtesy Laboratory Archives, Los Alamos National Laboratory)

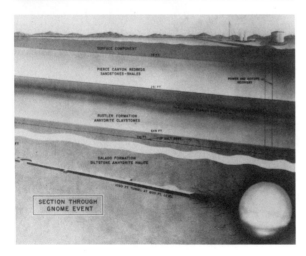

29 A Trip to the North Pole

In the mid-1960s I served on the scientific advisory committee to the Defense Intelligence Agency (DIA). It was chaired by Jack Howard, a vice-president at the Sandia National Laboratory in Albuquerque. We examined various programs sponsored by or contributing information to the DIA. One of our more interesting assignments involved a visit in the fall of 1968 to Ice Island, known as T-3, one of the enormous ice slabs that occasionally break off the Ellesmere ice shelf and float in the Arctic Ocean for years. It was about 3 miles wide and 25 miles long. At the time we visited it, T-3 was populated by wandering polar bears, seals, and a colony of twenty men, some of them employees of the DIA. The colony's announced purpose was to measure the plankton and fish population in the Arctic Ocean waters traversed by T-3. However, the DIA job was to count the population of Russian submarines that sat silent and vigilant under the Arctic Ocean sea ice. U.S. submarines also hid quietly under the ice. They were objects of interest to a similar colony of Russians on a neighboring ice island.

We flew to Elmendorf Air Force Base outside Anchorage and then to Eielson Air Force Base near Fairbanks. There we boarded a C-130 and went to Point Barrow at the edge of the Arctic Ocean. After a very cold night punctuated by a long session in a very hot sauna, our C-130 took off for T-3. The last living things I saw as we left Point Barrow were ravens, ubiquitous, highly intelligent, and resourceful birds in Alaska. T-3 was now floating at a point about 100 miles from the North Pole. The flight to the island was approximately 1,100 nautical miles.

The trip was gray and featureless, too cloudy to see the ice below us, the sky distinguished chiefly by a luminous glow where the sun hung forever, circling behind clouds on the low horizon.

We landed smoothly on the T-3 airstrip and stepped into a brisk wind and a temperature well below zero degrees Fahrenheit. We wore Arctic gear and were concerned mostly with protecting noses and faces from freezing. The C-130 propellers kept twirling. Engines remained on throughout our stay. The whole party quickly congregated in a warm room in a building that looked exceptionally sturdy considering its foundation on ice. It sheltered a deep hole through the ice to the ocean below. The research people used the hole for making their observations of sea life and to catch fish, mostly Arctic cod, for food. We saw rifles and were told that they were carried for protection against attack by visiting polar bears, chiefly interested in raiding the nearby garbage dump. There were rooms stocked with food and beer.

I soon learned that a particular level of security clearance for observing secret equipment had not been received for a few members of the party, including me. Jack and his more privileged cohort went off to a private area. Our group was named the Clear View Panel. "Clear Sky" was the term used by AFTAC to identify its global sampling network. T-3 would have been a uniquely valuable site for one of its sampling stations. In the exotic community of intelligence, it is quite possible that part of our mission to T-3 included a look by Jack and friends at the AFTAC installation. I didn't ask for an explanation nor was one given.

Those of us who remained began to trade stories. One of T-3's residents reminisced about a time when the Russian and American floes drifted very close to one another. The American colony decided to visit the Russians and stage a cocktail party. They set off across the sea ice with suitable food and beer for a few dozen guests, timing their arrival for the usual 5 PM party time. They were on Washington time. All time zones converge at the Pole and are indistinguishable. When the Americans arrived at the Russian floe, they discovered that the colony was on Moscow time, and the local clocks were now one hour past midnight the next day. However, the Russians were quickly wide-awake and eager to be good hosts. The party continued until there was nothing left to drink. It was much more in the spirit of the Arctic than of Washington where it would probably have triggered disciplinary action.

We decided we had time for a walk to the nearest edge of the floe. The residents checked our gear to make sure we wouldn't freeze and gave us rifles, saying that a visiting polar bear might mistake us for seals and attack. I don't know whether they were serious or just adding to the richness of our experience. In any case, I wasn't taught how to use the rifle I was carrying and, in case of a bear attack, would probably have swung it like a baseball bat.

The ice was crunchy but fairly smooth and the footage wasn't very difficult. We soon came on a snow-covered monument. It was the wreckage of a C-47, left there some years ago. If it were taking off for the mainland, it must have been loaded with fuel, perhaps overloaded unless the floe was a lot closer to Alaska than we were at the time. We examined the cockpit. It was in pristine shape. The problem appeared to be the undercarriage.

As we came close to the floe's edge we began climbing. We were on a pressure ridge, the buildup of crushed ice formed by the grinding of the sea ice against the freshwater ice of the floe. The top of the ridge was about fifteen feet above the floe surface. We walked down to the sea ice, thinking to extend our walk. However, it would have meant hopping from one moving plate to another and avoiding falling in between. We decided to turn back. The timing was good because the entire group was now gathering for the trip back to Point Barrow and Eielson.

Back at Eielson, Bill Ogle and I decided to drive into Fairbanks in the evening for dinner. A few miles short of town, Bill braked suddenly. A woman wearing only a long silver lamé dress, no coat, was waving frantically for a lift. She got in, thanked us, and asked to be dropped off at an address on the edge of town. We took her to a house ablaze with lights and echoing with loud music. She thanked us again and got out. We could only speculate about her problem.

We were due in Anchorage in three days and decided we had time to extend our trip from Eielson to take us through Valdez, a successor to Kodiak as a center for king-crab fishing. In order to get there we had to cross the Chugach Mountains just north of Valdez. With about fifty feet of powder per year, it's the snowiest part of the world, now available at a price to deep-powder lovers transported by helicopters. It was a lonesome, stormy, snowy, thrilling, and exhausting trip for us, but we were determined to see Valdez. As we slid from one side of the rather primitive road to the other, I kept reminding myself of the prospect of a king-crab dinner at the other end. Thompson Pass was the last obstacle. Valdez lay only a few miles beyond its southern foot. We reached the edge of town and followed signs to a restaurant that advertised seafood. Unfortunately, it was reserved for a wedding party, but they gave us directions to the only other restaurant in town, a short distance away. Valdez was not a large metropolis.

The second restaurant also specialized in seafood. We were shown by an attractive waitress to a rustic table with a spotless white tablecloth. There were only a few other customers. We guessed that most of Valdez was at the wedding party. All was well.

When the waitress came to take our order, I immediately said, "King crab." She said, "I'm sorry. We don't have crab today. The boats didn't come in." She turned to Bill who ordered cod. No problem. I was staring at the menu, trying to come to grips with reality. She turned to me. I said, "Did the boats come in yesterday?" She said, "Yes." I said, "Did they have crab?" "Yes." "Is there any left?" "You don't want *yesterday's* crab?" She was incredulous, as though I was ordering old Dungeness crab on Fisherman's Wharf in San Francisco. "Yes!" She shrugged. After a while she returned with a very large plate piled high with ice-cold, never-frozen king crab. It was apparently reserved for the cats we saw wandering around. It was the best king crab I have ever had, and I spent the evening demolishing the entire plate. Even the indifferent white wine went well with my once-in-a-lifetime treat.

30 Down the Aleutian Islands to Amchitka

The lab was constructing a site to conduct large thermonuclear tests at Amchitka, an island close to the end of the Aleutian chain off Alaska. Bill Ogle and I arrived in Anchorage in time to join Norris Bradbury, the lab director, and Bob Campbell, our field-engineering director. We were booked on the Reeve Airline for a flight down the Aleutians to the test site. On departure morning we were ushered to four seats reserved for us in the back of the plane opposite the lavatory. It was Monday and the plane was packed with Amchitka employees returning to work after a weekend of R&R in Anchorage. One of them was locked in the lavatory and refused to come out for take-off. The attractive, rather petite attendant kicked in the locked lavatory door and emerged holding a six-foot bruiser in a hammerlock. His pants were down around his knees and he was quite drunk. She dropped him into his seat, fastened his belt, and the plane immediately rolled for takeoff.

The attendant visited with us after we gained altitude. She was Janice Reeve, daughter of Bob Reeve, the airline owner. We were impressed with Janice, Bill Ogle most of all. The lab lost one of its great employees when Bill eventually quit his job at Los Alamos, left his New Mexico family, moved to Anchorage, married Janice, and went to work for Reeve Airline.

Amchitka was one the most enjoyable places I have ever visited on the job. It was a wildlife preserve, about thirty-five miles long and three miles wide. Bob Campbell took us to the camp garbage dump just before a truck arrived. We counted twenty-eight bald eagles patiently waiting for lunch. I guess Bob was politically conservative. He said that the eagles were a great American symbol, completely hooked on government handouts.

There was a big cove on one side of the island. It was covered with a kelp bed dotted with sea otters lying on their backs and eating sea urchins and abalone. They cracked shells by hammering them on flat rocks placed on their bellies. They were so numerous that it was hard to believe they had almost gone extinct when being heavily harvested by the Russians for their fur. I recently learned the sad news that the otter population in the Aleutians has decreased in recent years to about 10 percent of what it was in the 1960s.

You had to be careful when trying to walk around much of the island. It was covered with spongy tundra carved up with almost invisible, leg-breaking channels full of running seawater and Dolly Varden trout. Without any warning, fierce squalls would sweep over the island. While on a long walk, I took refuge from one by running to one of the scattered, falling-down hutments left by U.S. wartime occupation troops. As I crouched behind the largest standing wall, a bird the size of a big chicken landed at my feet. It crouched and looked up at me. It was a snowy ptarmigan. When the squall let up, it immediately took off.

31 The Oklo Natural Reactor

By a quirk of fate, I was reconnected with the invention of the chain-reacting pile in 1972, thirty years after the Fermi reactor first achieved criticality at Chicago. The occasion was the announcement in late 1972 that French scientists had discovered a natural reactor in a very rich uranium deposit at Oklo, Gabon, almost bordering the Congo to the south. At first I didn't believe it. How could nature have found it so easy to make a reactor when we found it so difficult? Then I learned that the reactor had operated nearly two billion years ago. The fissionable isotope uranium-235 decays with a much shorter half-life than uranium-238. It was more than four times as abundant two billion years ago than it is now. As a result, when a very rich and very thick vein of uranium ore was formed and when water surrounded the vein, as was the case at Oklo, it became possible for a chain reaction to occur spontaneously. It is an unofficial maxim in science that, given enough time, anything that is possible in nature will eventually happen. The Oklo reactor obeyed the maxim.

Accompanied by French scientists, I went to Oklo to learn more about this amazing event. It became an object of study for many years. One of its interesting properties was that, in spite of its age and the fact that water flowed through it, not only the uranium but most of the fission products and plutonium formed in uranium-238 remained in place.

I arrived at Libreville, the capital of Gabon, and was met at the airport by a driver in a long, black Mercedes limousine who took me to Le

Dialogue, at that time a luxury hotel. I continued to see the Mercedes parked outside the hotel. It remained there during my entire stay. I wasn't told that the car and chauffeur had been assigned to me. I hailed cabs to go to appointments. When I left Libreville, I was asked why I never used my Mercedes.

A few colleagues from the States had arrived earlier and joined me on my first night for dinner. The background music was by Bach. The remarkable menu was based on the daily delivery of choice items from Paris. The wine list was distinguished. The service was impeccable. The restaurant deserved at least a two-star Michelin rating. I was delighted, never expecting to find such splendor in an African city sitting squarely on the Equator.

We were invited to a reception at the Maison Blanc, the residence of President Albert Bongo. It became a sit-down dinner with an endless supply of wine and food. We were serenaded by an orchestra, the all-male musicians dressed semiformally. Then the dancing began. One of the attractive native female employees from the French Embassy asked me to dance. I couldn't resist a Viennese waltz and did a few turns.

The wine and toasting continued until midnight. Suddenly the musicians stripped down to loincloths and began to play wild "jungle" music dominated by percussion. The lovely French Embassy females reappeared wearing only native skirts and gyrating to the new tempo. One of them grabbed my hand and pulled me onto the dance floor. I clumsily tried to hold the deafening beat. The scientists from Paris and Saclay who had flown in to accompany us to Oklo were photographing the entire scene. Some weeks later when I visited them in Paris they were eager to show me the pictures. I didn't ask for copies and hope that they have now entirely disappeared.

After a few days in Libreville, we flew to Oklo. Sitting in the open-pit mine, we listened to talks in French and English about the origin of the deposit. The stability of the unprotected ancient reactor was of great interest to us. The favored storage technology for radioactive wastes in the United States is vitrification in which the wastes are incorporated in glass rods. The rods are placed within inert metal containers that will impede any leakage of radioactivity to the outside environment for thousands of years. The containers will be stored in underground vaults. In contrast, the Oklo reactor survived because uranium oxide is so insoluble that it has remained in place for approximately two billion years despite its exposure to mobile water. To date, the Department of Energy has not proceeded with any effort to incorporate waste products in highly insoluble oxides despite the fact that, on a time scale of millennia, glass is noticeably soluble.

Next to the deposits in Gabon, the uranium discoveries in northern Australia, east of Darwin, were the world's richest known deposits and among the oldest. I went there in 1976 with a colleague to examine cores that averaged 40 percent uranium content, candidates for a chain reaction similar to that at Oklo. However, unlike Oklo, the ore contained significant amounts of neutron-absorbing impurities, particularly boron and rare earths. We sampled a number of cores but were unable to find evidence of a prehistoric natural reactor. The favorable conditions at Oklo may prove to be unique. In succeeding years a number of additional reactor zones have been identified in the Oklo lode as mining continued in subsurface tunnels.

I described the Oklo reactor in an article in the July 1976 issue of *Scientific American* and in the 1978 yearbook of the Encyclopedia Britannica. Oklo attracted considerable attention in the academic community. I was invited to join the American Chemical Society national lecture tour for two years. After speaking at about two dozen campuses and ACS chapters all over the country, I decided that I had exhausted the subject and quit. I am told that the articles continue to be lecture subjects in nuclear physics and chemistry classes.

32 Disposal of High-Level Radioactive Wastes

The containment of radioactive debris in underground deposits became a major concern of radiochemists when the first underground test of a nuclear device was conducted at the Nevada Test Site in September 1957. Underground testing became the rule in 1962. The chief concern initially was to prevent the escape of radioactive nuclides either by prompt venting or by bursts of hot gases during drillback to recover diagnostic samples. But attention was soon focused on assuring that radioactive debris remained totally confined to the test site and posed no threat to potable water in inhabited areas outside the site. We conducted extensive tests designed to determine the migration rate of potentially harmful nuclides. Our measurements indicated that the debris remained wholly in place, partly because the melted soil that contained the debris was highly insoluble and partly because the desert contained little or no groundwater.

Our experience with containment of debris attracted the attention of people concerned with the disposal of commercial radioactive wastes. Various ways to dispose of wastes were being considered, including surface containment, deep geologic burial, ocean burial, and firing wastes into space. By the beginning of the 1970s a consensus emerged on the use of disposal in favorable geologic sites. I was increasingly consulted on our experience with Nevada debris.

In 1980 I joined a study panel on geologic waste disposal sponsored by the DOE and the National Research Council of the National Academy of Science. It was chaired by Professor Thomas Pigford, a faculty member at the University of California. We were charged to review the alternative technologies proposed for isolation of wastes from commercial nuclear power reactors, to evaluate their relative performance benefits, and to identify appropriate criteria for choosing among them that would limit maximum public exposure over thousands of years to a small fraction of existing natural radiation. The disposal of wastes produced by the military was left to the armed forces.

Earlier studies had recommended against surface storage. It would rely on ongoing surveillance for centuries, presumably an unethical burden if placed by us on succeeding generations. Deep geologic isolation in sealed chambers, reminiscent of ancient Egypt, offered an apparent solution to this problem. Preliminary recommendations included vitrifying wastes in borosilicate glass, packaging the resulting glass rods in long-lived containers, and surrounding the containers with additional absorbent materials. The panel assumed that the principal pathway to the environment would be by release of radioactive material to groundwater followed by transport of contaminated groundwater to the biosphere. Therefore control of release rates depended on delaying contact with water, slowing dissolution of radionuclides and release from the waste package, increasing groundwater travel time to the biosphere, increasing absorption of radionuclides in the geologic medium, and dispersing and diluting the radionuclides.

The final report, "A Study of the Isolation System for Geologic Disposal of Radioactive Wastes," contains over 350 pages of detailed information, including the need for further laboratory and field measurements concerning each of the aforementioned processes. Despite many uncertainties, the report concludes that it should be possible to design a geologic repository that would hold release rates over all relevant time to a level that would expose nearby people to much less than 10 percent of their exposure to natural radiation.

By signing the report, I affirmed my agreement with its favorable conclusions. I had no doubt about our ability to protect the environment by containment at the burial site. Nevertheless, I had serious reservations. My confidence that containment could be successful was based largely on what we knew about the properties of possible containers, for example, titanium alloys and various long-lived overpacks. I had considerably less confidence in our predictions concerning the integrity of the geologic environment. They required assumptions, never fully verifiable, concerning the crack-free, monolithic behavior of something like a cubic mile of surrounding basalt, granite, or tuff. The report neglected the need for transportation to select, remote geological environments and the possibility, however small, of accidents during transport. Opponents of nuclear power would certainly not overlook this aspect of geologic storage.

I strongly favored containment at the source of the wastes. It should be possible to safely store wastes at each of the sites where they are produced. In any case, each production site already has to provide expensive interim surface storage in water-cooled tanks for decades of decay of the shorter-lived nuclides. Why not also require suitable permanent, demonstrably safe storage nearby? I felt that since the most reliable and sufficient barriers were provided at the source, deep disposal was unnecessary and would actually weaken the case for safe disposal. Licensing would certainly be challenged by opponents and brought to a court of law. I would much rather defend the case if it relied on the complete integrity and continued surveillance of the closed-in environment.

Senator Pete Domenici, our then senior senator from New Mexico, frequently turned to scientists at Los Alamos for technical advice. In an invited conversation in his office following issuance of the panel's report, I mentioned my somewhat contrarian views. Sometime later he brought me to Washington to testify at a Senate committee hearing on geologic disposal. My testimony included a description of what I believed to be the merits of assured containment at the source. DOE experts presented detailed plans for deep geologic containment. They were obviously not receptive to my suggestions.

Now, twenty-five years later, deep geologic containment has been universally adopted by the many nations that have built nuclear power reactors. None of them has actually completed the construction of a permanent repository, and wastes have been placed only in some pilot test facilities. The Yucca Mountain site in Nevada was designated as the official U.S. deep-disposal site in 1987. It was planned to begin operation in 2010. The Yucca Mountain storage facility has been abandoned.

Expenditures by DOE on high-level waste disposal continue at a level of about $500 million a year. The money is largely provided by an almost invisible tax on the nuclear power portion of every electric utility bill. Delays in meeting scheduled performance targets are common. The ongoing appropriations testify to the good intentions of DOE but contain no significant penalties for postponements. Meanwhile, interim cooling tanks at production sites have by now provided generations-long storage.

Utility companies are calling urgently for increased local storage capacity. Plans are now being made for the nation to rely much more heavily on nuclear power. This will require even greater interim storage capacity. If the date for Yucca Mountain storage continues to be extended, I predict that permanent storage at large numbers of production sites will become national policy.

33 The Solar Neutrino Program

While I was at Los Alamos, I believed that the lab's richest source of new and stimulating information was our constantly refreshed pool of young, brilliant postdoctoral fellows, most of them specializing in theoretical physics. Wick Haxton joined this group with the award of a particularly distinguished J. R. Oppenheimer Fellowship in 1977. At the expiration of his appointment he was made a staff member and remained at Los Alamos until 1985. I was greatly impressed by the breadth and depth of his scientific interests. We became good friends and colleagues. In subsequent years he went on to a professorship at the University of Washington and gained international recognition for his research accomplishments.

Wick came to Los Alamos with an interest in the anomalously low solar neutrino flux values being reported by Brookhaven Laboratory scientist Ray Davis. The Davis value was less than one-half that predicted by standard models for the Sun's thermonuclear energy production.

The neutrino has no charge and only a minuscule mass. It rarely interacts with matter although it is second only to photons in particle abundance. The flux of neutrinos at the Earth, generated mostly by thermonuclear reactions at the center of the Sun, is the only observable measure of the level of activity in the Sun's core. A change in level would be followed by a change in observable surface luminosity but only after a delay of 1,000 years. Was the Davis anomaly suggesting a decreased level of core burning in advance of a change in luminosity?

Attempts to explain Ray's results became a major scientific activity in the 1970s and 1980s. An eventual explanation of this anomaly, discovery of a property called neutrino oscillation, led to Ray's award of a Nobel Prize.

Soon after his arrival at Los Alamos, well before the solar neutrino anomaly had been explained, Wick sought me out and suggested that we collaborate in searching for ways to measure solar neutrinos by their interaction with various target elements. In the early 1980s we published several papers that explored the potential value of such measurements. Our speculations led to a very ambitious proposal to measure the production of technetium-98 over the past several million years by absorption of solar neutrinos in molybdenum-98. The experiment would provide unique, highly valuable information about possible variations in the Sun's performance over millions of years. The measurement would require finding a deeply buried ore body of molybdenite that was being commercially mined. We identified a suitable mine, the Henderson mine operated by the AMAX Minerals Company at Red Mountain in Clear Creek County, Colorado. The ore was concentrated there and shipped to a processing plant at Fort Madison, Iowa.

Before they could host our experiment, the operators of the Colorado and Iowa facilities needed approval from their parent company, AMAX, located in Greenwich outside New York City. The chairman of AMAX, Pierre Gousseland, invited me to talk at a board meeting in Greenwich. Our plans had already been extensively discussed by numbers of international leaders in solar neutrino research and were receiving wide encouragement and support. We received a friendly reception by the AMAX board and were assured of the company's cooperation.

A number of people in the radiochemistry group, supervised by Ernest Bryant and Kurt Wolfsberg, attacked the numerous problems associated with separating a minuscule one hundred million atoms of technetium-98 from ten thousand tons of ore. We could think of no historical precedents. John Bahcall, generally recognized as the foremost expert in solar neutrino physics, called it a heroic effort. We arranged to set up a separation stage in the processing stream at Fort Madison and brought it online in late 1985. The first samples were carried back to Los Alamos for analysis in 1986. Unfortunately, the initial ionization efficiency of our mass spectrometer proved to be too low to provide useful statistics at mass 98. There were also significant background problems at Fort Madison due to recent roasting of a shallow ore deposit containing cosmic ray-induced technetium.

I became involved with starting the Santa Fe Institute at this time. I moved my office to Santa Fe and officially retired from laboratory employment in 1988. Funding for basic research was sharply decreasing, and members of the radiochemistry group, including the mass spectrometer people, turned their attention to more programmatic needs with assured financial support. Thus, the monumental effort that had gone into producing samples of separated technetium ground to a halt in 1988.

I considered this experiment one of the most ambitious and significant initiatives we had ever undertaken. Our failure to complete it was a deep disappointment. It vividly illustrated the importance of management decisions in the pursuit of basic scientific research when research funding competes directly with more applied programs. The problem is similar to management of a financial investment portfolio. The management philosophy can range all the way from emphasis on assured, relatively low rates of return to positive returns in 10 percent or less of the portfolio. However, with good management judgment, returns on 10 percent of a high-risk portfolio will be sufficiently rich that they more than compensate for the failures. Investment managers who are skilled in selecting high-risk, high-return initiatives, usually venture capital entrepreneurs, are uncommon and highly rewarded. There are too few counterparts in science, even in corporate labs that are also generally risk-averse.

Most individual basic science researchers don't have a diversified portfolio. They focus on a particular set of interests. The diversification problem usually falls within the province of basic science management. The bias is almost invariably in favor of assured, relatively low returns that can be achieved without a need for high, front-end investment. Large projects usually require political skills to produce line-item authorization in Washington for expensive instrumentation.

34 Atmospheric Dynamics Around Antarctica

In the early 1980s I retired from administrative duties and was given the title of Laboratory Senior Fellow. I joined a group of a half-dozen people with no formal responsibilities other than to talk with one another, occasionally with the laboratory director, and to pursue our various research interests. I was also a member of the White House Science Council and made frequent trips to its meetings in Washington. It was a job that made me rethink the future of science. Natural science, central to my entire career, was becoming less important on the national scene. I was nearing retirement age and viewed it as an opportunity to become a student again.

In late 1983 I was asked to serve as an advisor on a meteorological survey in the Antarctica and promptly accepted. However, I needed to undergo a thorough physical examination to demonstrate that, at an age approaching 64, I was unlikely to present an urgent medical problem in the Antarctic. I passed my examination with good marks, and in mid-December I was in Christchurch, New Zealand, waiting for a ski-equipped navy C-130 to take me to McMurdo Station. There was no fixed time of departure. My group had to be ready to leave a few hours after McMurdo notified Christchurch that the weather was favorable and would remain that way for the next twelve hours or so.

Members of the group were carrying equipment necessary to release a unique form of methane near the Antarctic continent and to measure its transport and dispersion as a function of time. In the early 1970s I had proposed the use of a synthetic methane with a mass of 21, compared to the abundant natural methane mass of 16, as a benign, nonradioactive atmospheric tracer. We demonstrated its practical utility by releasing some in the western United States and following its flow across the country until it reached the East Coast. The work is described in an article in *Science* published in March 1976 with the title "Heavy Methanes as Atmospheric Tracers."

I first decided to pursue the notion of synthesizing and using heavy methane as a tracer when I noticed that the summary of an exhaustive analysis of all the gases in a heavy, persistent smog over the Los Angeles area contained no gas with a mass of 21. On further investigation I was surprised to find that there is no detectable amount of any gas in nature with this mass number. But it was possible to synthesize methane with mass 21. A molecule of methane contains one atom of carbon and four atoms of hydrogen. If it is made with one atom of the rare heavy carbon isotope of mass 13 and four atoms of rare deuterium with mass 2, the molecular mass is 21. It is also true that ammonia, with one atom of nitrogen and three atoms of hydrogen, could be synthesized with the rare nitrogen isotope of mass 15 and three deuterium atoms. It would have a mass of 21 and could be used in many interesting research applications. Surprisingly, I have never seen a reference to its use in research with fertilizer uptake or any other application.

The group bound for the Antarctic had a major interest in atmospheric dynamics in that part of the world. Methane-21 appeared to be an ideal tracer. Its release at a particular point in space and time would permit us to track the fate of that part of the atmosphere over many thousands of miles. The analysis required the collection of a large volume of air at any desired location, the separation of methane, which exists in the atmosphere at a concentration of about two parts per million, and the measurement of its isotopes by analysis in a gas mass spectrometer. All of these capabilities existed. The detection sensitivity for stable methane-21 was comparable to that for any of the radioactive isotopes we constantly monitored.

So here we were in Christchurch waiting to release methane-21 over Antarctica. Anything having to do with the atmospheric dynamics of this continent is of general scientific interest, but the principal motivation for this particular project was rather different. There had been rumors of bomb testing in the Antarctic Ocean, presumably from a ship or submarine base, and people in Washington wanted to know under what atmospheric conditions a sampling station at McMurdo or at the South Pole would intercept debris from various points around the Antarctic.

While we waited we sampled New Zealand cuisine. Breakfasts with lots of fresh fruit were very good. Dinners were not great. Very young lamb was presumably reserved for export. There was a plentiful supply of mutton that we mostly ignored. Searching the Christchurch restaurants, we could occasionally find a good steak and a drinkable red wine. The beer was excellent.

The town of Christchurch was lovely. I particularly admired the trees that were on display in a park dedicated to New Zealand's many fascinating varieties. The buildings were in the attractive tradition of British university towns.

We were outfitted with standard Antarctic gear, much too warm in the New Zealand summer. We waited patiently. Weather at McMurdo was bad. New Year's Day came and went. We were now in year 1984. Then the long-expected message arrived. Present yourself at the airstrip at ten hundred! A few hours later we were boarding our C-130. Except for the skis hung on the undercarriage, the plane was familiar. The crew of three was not. The pilot and copilot were female. So was the cargo handler. My first impression was that they were all recruited by a Hollywood casting studio. They looked and acted almost too perfect for their parts. As it turned out, they were exceptionally good at every aspect of their job.

Christchurch is 2,400 miles from McMurdo. Our flight time was a little over seven and one-half hours, long enough for us to fall into brief naps. C-130s are extremely noisy and everyone is supposed to wear earplugs. They interfere with conversation. The monotony was not broken by interesting scenery. We flew almost entirely over open ocean until ice floes and icebergs appeared, finally consolidating into the Antarctic Ice Sheet. It became the almost unbroken Ross Ice Shelf as we let down for landing at the Ross Island strip.

Bob Jeffries, the air transport manager at Los Alamos, and I were assigned a shared room in one of the dormitories. We collected our bags and were driven to our new home, a ramshackle, prefab building. The streets at the Station were ice-free and muddy. There was no obvious design plan in the collection of structures that make up the Station. Everything was flown in as needed and assembled. Concrete block foundations were common. Builders avoided pouring concrete at local temperatures. The exigencies of life in Antarctica meant that little or no attention had been paid to aesthetics.

Our first bad impressions got worse as we found our assigned room. It was filthy. We set our bags in the hallway, found mops, pails of water, and some rag cloths, and went about cleaning the place. After two hours of hard work, it passed inspection and we moved in.

A note had been delivered from Paul Guthals, my liaison with our NSF and navy hosts. He was director of the overall meteorological experiment. He urged us to attend a reception at the station commander's navy quarters that evening. Bob and I found the building and presented ourselves. Paul was somehow mistaken. It was a sit-down dinner and we were not among the invitees. However, we got over our initial embarrassment and stayed for a round of drinks. It was our first and last encounter with top navy management.

Our first full day was spent helping to set up and test equipment. As advisors and observers, Bob and I had a light load. The rest of our trip was largely spent on VIP visitor trips, mostly by navy helicopters. Permission to see Emperor penguins was granted only to bona fide researchers, but getting to a nearby large Adelie penguin colony was adequate compensation. We were immediately adopted by one of the penguins, who followed us around like a pet puppy during our entire stay. Not all the visitors to the colony were as friendly. South Polar skuas nested nearby and fed on penguin eggs and chicks. They kept landing at our feet, apparently asking for food, and, when none was offered, could suddenly become menacing, flying straight toward us with claws outstretched. We saw them often, and I quickly learned to heartily dislike them.

We spent two hours exploring Scott's Hut, built by Robert Scott in 1911 to support his expedition to the South Pole. He reached the Pole in January 1912, a month after Amundsen had gotten there, but he and his companions died on the way back. Everything in the hut is remarkably well preserved in the cold polar climate. The cans on the pantry shelves contain a variety of high-calorie food, also including tins of cabbage and onion. Their counterparts are probably still available in London markets.

We also visited the hut at nearby Cape Royds, built by Ernest H. Shackleton in 1909. It was restored by a New Zealand group in the

1950s. The contents are as well preserved as at the Scott hut, and the choices were much the same as Scott's.

Our group was joined by our C-130 pilots for a trip to the nearby New Zealand station. Their building rested on the shore of an ice-covered lake. It had a small expanse of open water and we were told that anyone who dived in would get a souvenir tee shirt. The only volunteers were the ladies who stripped down and dove in without a moment's hesitation. Cameras were forbidden. I wished I had their courage. The tee shirt would have been a great keepsake. We were all rewarded with tea and buttered hot scones by our hosts.

On another day-excursion we helicoptered up McMurdo Dry Valley, a region free of snow and ice for many miles inland. Air, constantly flowing down various deep valleys from the Pole, can lose all its moisture in some of them before reaching the sea. Our trip continued to higher altitudes where we encountered overhanging glaciers with steep, vertical walls. Our pilot approached an ice wall almost within rotor length, inspected the face and rose slowly all the way to the glacier top. We then descended back to the valley floor and landed. The transitions in scenery from the dry, dark valley floor to towering glaciers were the most dramatic of our entire trip.

We spent an afternoon on the Coast Guard 13,200-ton icebreaker *Polar Sea* as it opened a channel to McMurdo Station. We were transported in one of the ship's two helicopters. It settled onto the pad at the stern, and we were immediately taken in charge by two crewmembers. The *Polar Sea* and its twin, *Polar Star*, were the Coast Guard's newest and most powerful icebreakers at the time.

Soon after our arrival aboard the *Polar Sea*, the three independently powered shafts started turning, and the ship resumed its task of ramming a channel through the ice. The bow would rise several feet on the thick shelf and then crash through. The noise level was considerably higher than on a C-130, certainly over 100 decibels, and our conversation on deck depended heavily on gestures and sign language. This was complicated by my need to constantly grab the rail. We went midship and then climbed up to the bridge where normal conversation became possible.

The ship carried a crew of fifteen officers and 126 enlisted men. They possessed all the skills necessary to be isolated and completely self-sufficient in the Antarctic seas for months at a time. They were gregarious, great communicators, and highly competent. I suspect their selection was even more rigorous than that of the crew of a nuclear submarine.

The weather at the Pole was pronounced suitable, and we rejoined our C-130 and remarkable crew for the 800-plus-mile flight to the Scott-Amundsen base at the Pole. Much of the several-hour trip was spent taking pictures of glaciers, mountains of ice, and snowfields. We arrived in time to join about thirty support staff and researchers for lunch. It was a simple cafeteria meal distinguished by the fact that the post office opened and we could mail cards postmarked with our position. A little shop also opened and I bought a unique tee shirt, available only at the base. It said "SKI SOUTH POLE. 10,000 FEET OF BASE AND 1/2 INCH OF POWDER." Both numbers were a little on the high side.

After lunch we were given a short tour of the building and its Spartan living facilities. Then we went outside. I borrowed some skis and tried them out on the ice. The ground was level and there was nothing covering the trail that deserved to be called powder, but I was determined to ski the South Pole. Then we walked to the tall pole driven into the snow that marked the almost exact location of the true Pole. The slight error was due to the fact that the snowpack kept moving downhill toward the sea and the marker pole had to be relocated several feet in the ice every year. The obligatory pictures were taken.

I was attracted to a crew of Europeans who were drilling deep ice cores. A major technological challenge was keeping the borehole open because the pressure at depth is very high. It is countered by keeping the hole filled with pressurized, petroleum-based drilling fluid. Core drilling is a major activity at a number of sites in the Antarctic. The cores provide hundreds of researchers with enormous amounts of data concerning various meteorological, ecological, atmospheric, volcanic, and other histories of our planet over many thousands of years.

Our visit was short. The base was not equipped to house numbers of visitors, and the researchers were busy making the most of their limited time. We climbed into our C-130 and settled down for the trip back. On our arrival at McMurdo, the rest of the long day was spent packing for the trip back to Christchurch.

Once back in New Zealand, I interrupted my trip back to New Mexico for a day of trout fishing on North Island. My guide said his last client was President Jimmy Carter. We went to a beautiful, fast-flowing river emptying into Lake Taupo. The guide cast first, dropping a fly into an eddy behind a huge rock. He immediately hooked a large rainbow trout, about twenty-three inches, expertly brought it to our feet, and released it. I was awed. His only comment was, "It's scrawny." Was it possible that this was a pet trout who had been taught to take my guide's fly and impress tourists?

I had less success. To catch trout consistently on a fly, it's necessary to think like a trout. It was obvious by the end of the day that I didn't think like New Zealand trout. I once tried to explain this aspect of fly fishing to the great physicist I. I. Rabi who had never fly fished. He had to consider the notion of intelligence in fish. Then he smiled and said, "I see. It's a battle of wits."

35 The White House Science Council

In 1982 I accepted an appointment to the White House Science Council (WHSC) which would take me to Washington and elsewhere some part of each month. At the time I joined, the members, in addition to chairman Jay Keyworth, were Harold Agnew, Edward Teller, John Bardeen, Allen Bromley, Ed Frieman, Sol Buchsbaum, Art Karman, David Packard, Don Fredrickson, Edward Gray, Ed David, and Robert Hunter. Our task was to counsel the president, through Presidential Science Advisor Keyworth, on policy matters that had substantial scientific and technical content. It soon became clear that scientific factors mattered considerably less to the White House staff than political considerations.

The role of science in defining national policy had steadily decreased since the heady postwar days. When the Atomic Energy Commission was established to assure civilian control of nuclear weapons, it was managed by top-level scientists. Over the years the emphasis on weapons development and nuclear energy faded. The AEC was abolished in the mid-1970s. It was succeeded for a few years by the Energy Research and Development Administration (ERDA). As our supply of oil from the Arab countries became increasingly important and increasingly threatened, legislation was passed in 1977 that established the Department of Energy (DOE) to manage a comprehensive approach to the nation's energy problems. Innovative science was no longer high on its list of priorities.

The problems that the DOE had to deal with were far larger than its authorities or capabilities. When I joined the WHSC, the new Reagan administration was relying heavily on our national oil corporations and market forces to solve the problems of oil supply. The DOE, despite its legislative mandate, remained important but was not the major player.

I wondered then and even more now that no proposal appears to have ever been seriously pursued in Washington to establish a cabinet-level Department of Science and Technology. It would not displace the National Science Foundation as the principal patron of basic research but would emphasize stronger scientific direction and management of work on a number of increasingly urgent problems. Global warming is a current example. Scientists advise but have no major responsibilities for implementation. The legislative and administrative branches of government apparently have no great faith in the role of scientists as managers. I assume that they would oppose a Department of Science. A proposal to raise the EPA, largely composed of attorneys, to cabinet level failed. This inertia stands in sharp contrast to repeated public statements that "we need another Manhattan Project" to solve various urgent problems. But since the demise of the AEC there has been no constituency among scientists for an operational role in government. They would probably also actively oppose the idea.

President Reagan and his advisors certainly did not rely heavily on scientific or technological inputs. The NASA programs involved engineering more than science and were increasingly important to large aerospace companies in California. We listened to their plans for placing an orbiting laboratory in space. We unanimously recommended that instrumentation should be developed for an unmanned laboratory that would automatically make all planned observations and download information back to earthbound scientists. NASA and the administration favored less scientifically demanding but much more expensive manned spaceships. We were told that Congress would never vote to fund the project if there were no people aboard. Our advice was withdrawn. I'm not sure that it is even a matter of record.

I got a minor but particularly interesting assignment while on the WHSC as a result of the strike by the Professional Air Traffic Controllers (PATCO) that started in August 1981 and eventually failed after most of the strikers were fired by order of the president. Commercial air traffic continued at close to its normal levels despite the absence of about three-fourths of the controllers. They were replaced in part by supervisors, but the number of controllers was sharply down from the prestrike levels. Shortly after I joined the WHSC, we were told that the president was concerned that the shortage of controllers might be increasing the risk of air travel. The president wanted any members of the Council who had pilot licenses to sit on the flight deck during their commercial travel and offer their opinions and those of the pilots they talked to about the adequacy of the lightly manned traffic control system. I was a licensed pilot and volunteered. A few days later I received a letter signed by the president requesting that the crew captain allow me to sit on the flight deck if he approved my suitability, principally meaning that I had not been drinking and seemed physically fit.

I joined the flight crews on several domestic flights, usually with TWA, on my trips between Albuquerque and Washington. The trips were uneventful. The periods of chief interest were climb-outs and descents to assigned altitudes and final approaches, particularly coming into Washington over the Potomac in poor visibility and heavy traffic. I remember one event involving the sudden appearance of a helicopter off our wing and several hundred feet below us. I was told that these apparent intrusions happened rather frequently on approaches to busy airports but that the helicopter pilots were safety conscious and generally stayed close to their assigned altitudes and outside the approach lanes. Pilots were not supposed to make independent judgments about neighboring traffic except in emergencies to avoid collisions.

I always felt quite safe on commercial flights. I would have felt even safer if the pilots had full information from their own radar concerning neighboring traffic and were allowed to manage their routine departures and arrivals with minimal assistance from ground-based control. However, they were not allowed to use available technology that would tell them about neighboring aircraft or traffic spacing.

In the 1980s radar systems for ground-based traffic control were still dependent on hard-tube computer technology that was long obsolescent. The FAA seemed incapable of successfully modernizing their technology despite spending very large sums of money on systems that didn't work. I shared the common opinion that professional pilots had about the competence of the FAA bureaucracy. It wasn't high.

The major contributions of ground-based traffic control are during landings in highly unfavorable weather conditions and in management of traffic on the runways. Doppler radar can detect dangerous downdrafts that might slam aircraft into the ground on final approach. My report recommended its installation at every busy airport. I believe that this recommendation was slowly adopted and is now generally implemented.

In 1982 we were briefed on the existence of GPS, the global positioning system, described as accurate enough to guide a missile through a window. The technology was highly classified and limited to military use. It was immediately clear that the system had many important potential uses in civilian life, the most obvious one being for the navigation of commercial aircraft. We asked whether it was possible to declassify a civilian version of the military system. We wrote a report that Jay Keyworth used to support the proposal in a letter to the president. A few months later President Reagan issued a directive to the DOD to make a degraded version of GPS available to the public.

One day I was called from Washington on a highly secure phone line and asked to fly to London immediately to meet Jay Keyworth concerning an urgent problem that he would explain to me when we met overseas. We were a group of four when we gathered at an inn outside London. We met a man who told us that he could turn water into motor fuel with a simple additive. We were there to investigate his claim because someone with important connections to the White House was financially supporting this vital invention. The inventor was driving a shiny new Jaguar. After a briefing, he drained the gasoline from the Jaguar and refilled the tank with "treated" water that we smelled and tasted in advance. It had a small trace of methanol, a mysteriously necessary minor ingredient. As he filled the tank, I detected an odor close to the fill tube. It was the odor of methanol but much too strong to be due to the water we had just examined. I know of nothing else that smells like methanol. During the Prohibition Era it was commonly referred to as "wood" alcohol and was often sold to unsuspecting alcoholics who were then in danger of losing their eyesight.

We piled into the car and went for a very high-speed ride. The engine ran smoothly. Back at our hotel, I reported that I believed that the car was fueled with methanol from a second tank. I had to defend my conclusion vigorously. My certainty was partly due to the fact that the claimed invention was thermodynamically impossible.

Many months later I was summoned to Dallas by the office of the U.S. District Attorney to testify as an expert witness at a criminal trial. Some wealthy Dallas oil people had invested a large sum of money in the water-to-gasoline process and were now charging the inventor, our mutual friend from the United Kingdom, with fraud. The topic was no longer unmentionably top secret. I testified that, to the best of my belief, the demonstration I had witnessed in England involved the substitution of methanol for water. The defense attorney, the famous Boston criminal lawyer F. Lee Bailey, had somehow obtained a long list of my security clearances and questioned my ability to testify openly on a matter of such vital importance to the nation's security. I learned later that the inventor was acquitted. The experience reminded me again that the conclusions I reach, based on what appears to be obvious hard evidence, do not necessarily convince nonscientists. The world of physical reality, the world in which I have made my living, is much more constrained than the world of most of my fellow humans.

Disagreements can occur even among scientists looking at the same evidence. A well-known example occurred during my WHSC tenure. President Reagan wanted an alternative to the doctrine of mutual assured destruction (MAD), the notion that an attack with nuclear weapons on the United States, presumably by the U.S.S.R., would be answered with nuclear weapons. He didn't know of any acceptable alternative military response and became convinced that development of an impenetrable umbrella over the entire country, a technology that could then be shared with the Russians and other nations, would lead to the dismantling of nuclear weapons. In any case it would deter a hostile missile attack.

Edward Teller, a fellow member on the Council and an ardent proponent of strategic defense, told President Reagan of an important breakthrough in laser design by a scientist at Livermore. This information may have helped the president decide to launch the Strategic Defense Initiative (SDI) that he announced on national TV on March 23, 1983. He delivered his address from the White House before a group of dinner guests that included Teller, some other members of the WHSC, and Hans Bethe and Victor Weisskopf, skeptics about the practicality of

SDI. The new initiative was quickly dubbed Star Wars by the popular press.

Gorbachev was passionately opposed to Star Wars and repeatedly asked for its abandonment. I suppose that he felt it would lead to a pre-emptive attack on Russia. Very influential advisors in his government insisted that adequate Russian resources were available to develop a similar shield. But if he followed this advice, Gorbachev would have to give his military more support and allocate less to meeting already desperate domestic needs. He resisted and continued his opposition to SDI throughout the Reagan administration and into the succeeding Bush administration. Reagan's insistence on preserving SDI, despite any evidence of success, torpedoed repeated counterproposals by Gorbachev to sharply cut back on nuclear weapons stockpiles and eventually eliminate them. But Russian domination of Eastern Europe declined and Gorbachev left the corridors of power. Reagan's faith in the fantasy of an impenetrable shield against missiles is widely believed to have been a contributing factor to Russia's demise. Historians will probably favor a much more complicated view.

At some point in 1982 we were briefed on a puzzling new disease that was showing up in the gay community and resulting in deaths. The Centers for Disease Control was beginning to be alarmed. We were uncertain about the priority of this subject on the WHSC agenda. Our guidance was informal. It seemed to be, "It's only gays. Don't be alarmed unless you have a personal reason."

I asked my fellow panel member, David Packard, founder and chairman of Hewlett-Packard and an old hand in Washington, what sort of scientific advice he felt was valuable to an administration that was so highly focused on its social and political agenda. The answer was, "Study their agenda." Despite the fact that it obviously wasn't included in the WHSC charter, if such a charter even existed, I was attracted to this notion. It reminded me of my earlier days with the Aspen Institute and added legitimacy to involving physical science with the complexity and inelegance of human affairs. David was saying, in effect, we should broaden our own agenda. Surely C. P. Snow would approve.

36 Simplicity and Complexity

Back in Los Alamos I returned to my concern with the direction that physical science should take. Why do we do physics? Perhaps it's related to the fact that our love of stories is innate. We go to movies, watch TV, read history, biographies, and fiction, and exchange accounts of our experiences with our friends. I think of these mental activities as falling into three classes. We commonly construct "snapshots" that describe static objects and situations. We recount histories of past events that are the stuff of "movies." Less commonly and with much more difficulty we attempt to predict the future. We even read horoscopes.

Physics is a form of storytelling. We look for patterns in things or events and construct snapshots. Since our interest is usually in the dynamics of a process, we attempt to describe its behavior in terms of a differential equation or set of equations. The "movie" is the integrated solution solved over many frames. When physicists make their movies, they frequently deal with classical mechanics and use equations. The equations that describe the movement of planets around the Sun can be expressed to a very close approximation in a simple form. The mass of the Sun is so large that it governs each planet's orbit. The other planets have essentially zero effect on each other. Therefore Newton had to solve the relatively simple two-body problem and analytically produce "movies" that could predict the future with great precision for any body in our solar system.

About half the stars in our galaxy belong to binary star and multiple star systems. Usually the movement of two massive stars around one another can be described with relatively simple two-body mathematics. However, the movement of planets in a binary star system would require a mathematical description involving multibody differential equations. There would be no analytical solution, none of the elegance of Newtonian classical mechanics. Planetary mechanics in a binary star system would, at least in principle, be complex. Precise long-term solutions would no longer be possible. The fate of the planets in such systems could have many possible outcomes. If Newton had been born in a binary star system, he would have had to deal immediately with complexity, not the simplicity of the two-body problem. The dynamics are nonlinear.

But once Newton discovered the simplicity of planetary motion in our solar system, scientists looked for it everywhere. Strangely enough, it seemed to be common. The assumption early in the last century that electrons were particles moving like planets around a heavy nucleus was a useful metaphor. It drove the development of the quantum mechanical description of atomic orbitals that specify the probability of electron positions around the nucleus. The fall of an apple dropping off a tree is said to have inspired Newton with the necessary notion of a force that acted on the apple. The orbit of the Moon around the Earth is a closely related two-body problem that provides us with a beautiful visual introduction to celestial mechanics. The sight of a pinpoint of light moving across the night sky, marking the passage of an artificial satellite, may not be as dramatic visually but is a relatively recent introduction to the simplicity of Newtonian motion.

Complexity became a major theme on Earth when life evolved. Life involves many variables and is, therefore, a multibody problem with nonlinear dynamics. Living systems are open, which means that they can disobey thermodynamic laws because they operate out of thermodynamic equilibrium with their surrounding environments. The behavior of any living system, interacting with its environment, cannot be predicted over long periods of time. The variability may be minimal if the environment is stable, as with relatively simple prokaryotic cells in oceans. It can be very high if the life form has an extensive memory and exists in variable environments. Human life is an extreme example of this kind of complexity.

Why did nature make life so complex? Much of the complexity seems overdone. Our bodies are constantly at work to hold variables within narrow limits. This internal regulatory function is called homeostasis. We expect our body temperature, pulse rate, and blood pressure to be reasonably constant. All complex systems have regulatory mechanisms that constrain variables. Societies are homeostatic. They have religions, custom, black magic, laws, and countless prescribed behavioral patterns that produce order out of what otherwise becomes chaotic and self-destructive. Ecologies evolve to quasi-equilibrium and incorporate homeostatic constraints. Much of our complexity seems to be on standby, to be called on when adjustments to changing environments are needed. Natural scientists approached biology as if it were simple, sometimes with considerable success. But they paid little if any attention to the complex relationships between natural and social phenomena and the world of human affairs. The intellectual world divided into specialized camps that more or less ignored one another.

In 1959 C. P. Snow began to write essays deploring the separation of academia into separate cultures. Academicians used the terms "hard" and "soft" sciences to distinguish natural science from social science. But in recent decades the mathematics of chaos and the ubiquity of computers have produced a convergence of interests between the cultures.

I became increasingly aware of the divergence of cultures in the 1950s when I was invited by Chicago industrialist and philanthropist Walter Paepcke to join some of his discussion groups in Aspen, Colorado. The participants in each group included about two dozen businessmen, politicians, academicians, and artists. I was the only natural scientist. The sessions were usually chaired by Mortimer Adler who developed an agenda centered on the list of Great Books he had prepared for students at St. John's College. The discussions might have been better led by Socrates, Aristotle, or Plato. I was probably the least prepared of the participants.

We were immersed in the world of the ancient Greek scholars. I was fascinated by the range of their inquiries. Their science was frequently off track but still enlightening with respect to many aspects of the search for broad understandings. I was drawn to the philosophy of Heraclites. His main theme was captured in two words: *"Panta rei."* Everything moves! Plato was static compared to Heraclites and the philosophy of dynamics.

ASPEN INSTITUTE FOR HUMANISTIC STUDIES

Founded by Walter P. Paepcke 1949   31 Jan – 5 Feb, '65

Public Understanding of the Role of Science in Society

ABOVE: I began to participate in seminars and study groups at the Aspen Institute in 1956 and, after repeated visits over several years, bought a second home there. These photographs are of fellow participants in a government-sponsored conference in early 1965 on "Public Understanding of the Role of Science in Society."

ABOVE: The Science Advisory Committee to the Department of Defense Intelligence Agency held regular meetings in the 1960s at the Air Force Technical Applications Center (AFTAC) located off the Beltway outside Washington. Left to right in the front row are Bill Ogle, head of the Los Alamos Test Division; myself; Jack Howard, vice-president of Sandia National Laboratories and chairman of the Committee; and Frank Thomas; back row, Allen Peterson, Stanford University and SRI; Eugene Herrin, Southern Methodist University; seismologist Bob Levin; and Jack Rosengren of Livermore National Laboratory.

LEFT: Participants in the April 1965 E. O. Lawrence Award ceremony were, left to right, John Lawrence, Arthur C. Upton, myself, Theodore Taylor, Floyd Culler, Milton Edlund, and chairman of the Atomic Energy Commission, Glenn Seaborg.

ABOVE: The Department of Defense Intelligence Agency Science Advisory Group boarding an Air Force C-130 in October 1968 for an inspection trip to a DIA installation on Fletcher Ice Island, also known as T-3, drifting in the Arctic Ocean about 280 miles from the North Pole.

LEFT: The *Anchorage Daily Times* report of the Air Force flight to Fletcher Ice Island. The major mission of the flight is not mentioned.

Anchorage Daily Times

ANCHORAGE, ALASKA, TUESDAY, OCTOBER 22, 1968

Ice Island — Where Is It?

a giant piece of gla-
7 billion tons of it —
the frigid waters of
Ocean.
population of 15 and
several "ice islands"
m Air Command has
t is.
Is known as T-3 or
station Bravo and is
aups 2, Fletcher's Ice

alar Lt. Colonel Jos-
letcher, the station's
meier, the island was
as a base for Arctic
ed weather reporting.
first station was es-
April 1952, the is-
roveled thousands of
nd the Arctic Ocean.
ent location is 280
the North Pole and
from Ft. Burrow on
m Arctic Slope.
ary behind Ice islands
ustan Air Command's
nd association with
n stations probably
ith when a giant piece
spotted during a rou
near Ellsmere Is-
is dubbed Target X
ing of such a large
is spurred the search
: Islands capable of
permanent or semi-
hilts for experiments-
c or military oper-

stanlier Island simi-
ct X was found. This
illed T-2 and the first
redesignated as T-1
s after hosting T-2
unt was located and

ands were claimed as
Islands" rather than
floes, the difference
r composition and
e.
on is normally 6 to 9
during the summer
feet thick in winter.
ubject to tremendous
rounding and breakup
Islands average 175
Navy. Previously when T-3

year the world received the first
Arctic weather report from T-3.
During 1965 the Air Force Cambridge Research Center re-es-
tablished the station for research purposes, this time for
only 144 days duration.
    The island was later reestab-
lished for its third occupation.
During this time core drillings
into the ice showed the island
to be composed of layers of ice,
rock, gravel and fossils dating
back 3,000 years. This indicated
a continental glacier formation.
Investigations later showed that
T-3 originally broke from the
giant glaciers of Ellesmere Island, northwest of Greenland.
    By 1957 this traveling island
had completed a tour of the Arctic Ocean and was once again
close to Ellesmere Island. On
October 12 the position of the
island was 85 degrees 18.8' N,
142 degrees 19.7' W, once again
placing it far north, only 250
miles from the North Pole.
    Recently, an Air Force C-130
Hercules known as "Inustlin'
Husky" by the crew, delivered
supplies and visitors to T-3.
    "Inustlin' Husky," one of 12
C-130 turbo-prop aircraft assigned to the 17th Tactical Air-
life Squadron at Elmendorf Air
Force Base, was the first Alas-
kan Air Command flight to land
on T-3 since 1961. The aircraft
was not ski-equipped, which is
rather unusual for winter flights
in the Arctic, according to Maj.
Igor P. Prokofieff, 17th Tactical
Airlift Squadron.
    The aircraft commander was
Col. Charles W. Johnson, Jr.,
commander of the 21st Compos-
ite Wing, parent unit of the 17th.
Johnson's crew consisted of
Maj. Walter H. Ott, Maj. John
O. Haley, Maj. Prokofieff, T-
Sgt. Thomas C. Sommerville, S-
Sgt. John B. Tippett, and Sgt.
Kenneth R. Browder.
    The 17th started making air-
drop resupply missions to the
summer at the request of the

ICE ISLAND — A SPOT ON THE MAP

The map shows the relative location of Fletcher's Ice Island T-3 in relation
Anchorage and the North Pole. The island is used for research purposes
since its discovery in 1950, has floated around the Arctic Ocean to its pre

ABOVE: A very rich deposit of uranium ore at Oklo, Gabon, supplied much of France's demand for fuel for its nuclear program. This is a picture of the open-pit Oklo mine taken in 1975. A wooden stage can be seen near the middle of the photo. It was occupied by Gabonese notables speaking at a ceremony celebrating the discovery of the Oklo natural reactor by French nuclear scientists in 1972. (Photograph reproduced courtesy of William J. Maeck)

ABOVE: An international audience attended the celebration of the natural reactor discovery. It consisted of French scientists involved in the discovery, journalists, and nuclear scientists and dignitaries from a number of other countries. (Photograph reproduced courtesy of William J. Maeck)

LEFT: Ranking members of the Gabon government addressed their guests at the Oklo ceremony. They described the establishment of an officially designated historic site at Oklo. All the proceedings were in French but an English translation was provided. (Photograph reproduced courtesy of William J. Maeck)

BELOW: The Oklo uranium deposit sloped diagonally downward. The post in this picture marks the bottom of the natural reactor zone. As open-pit mining proceeded this region became a platform high above the floor of the pit. Many more reactor zones have since been identified in the underground extension of the mining operation. (Photograph reproduced courtesy of William J. Maeck)

ABOVE: Attendees at the Oklo ceremony examined the mineralized zone and pocketed small, radioactive specimens from the rubble lying at their feet. My souvenir from this site is a black, oval rock, about an inch on a side, containing approximately 40 percent uranium oxide. This concentration lies at the exceptionally high end of known uranium ores. (Photograph reproduced courtesy of William J. Maeck)

BELOW: Roads in Gabon were few, primitive, and far between. The mined uranium ore from Oklo was carried by this aerial tram across the Gabon–Belgian Congo border to the banks of the Congo River and floated downriver by barge to freighters moored in the harbor at the river's mouth. (Photograph reproduced courtesy of William J. Maeck)

ABOVE: Mount Elbrus in Russia is the highest mountain in Europe. Its western summit peaks at 18,500 feet. A three-mile tunnel at its base leads to a unique neutrino experimental facility directly under the summit. I went there in 1987 to learn more about detection of neutrinos.

LEFT: I am standing at the entrance to the Mount Elbrus tunnel, about to take the railway car to the neutrino laboratory. When I asked for an estimate of the cost of building this tunnel, I was told that it was an unrecorded expenditure. I suspect that the same holds true for a considerable fraction of major Russian expenditures on scientific research.

ABOVE: John Holland, a major figure in complexity science, entertains a visiting group in the early 1990s at his home at the University of Michigan campus in Ann Arbor. The four visible figures in the photo are, from left to right, Murray Gell-Mann, Ken Arrow, me, and host John Holland.

ABOVE: Robert O. Anderson, then the country's largest individual landowner, became chairman of the SFI board in the early 1990s. He is shown here visiting with me in my office at the Institute's famous "convent" on Canyon Road in Santa Fe.

LEFT: Secretary of Energy James D. Watkins presents the Enrico Fermi Award for 1990 to me in a ceremony at the Department of Energy headquarters in Washington. This honor capped my professional career in physical science. I resigned my position as president of the Santa Fe Institute shortly after and began to work as a neophyte in neuroscience.

BELOW LEFT: My wife joined me in this picture taken at the Enrico Fermi Award ceremony. The gold medal, bearing a handsome likeness of Enrico Fermi, is not meant to be worn. It is 3 inches in diameter, a quarter-inch thick, and made from three-quarters of a pound of 14-carat gold from the Philadelphia Mint. I was also given a lapel-sized version of the medal.

RIGHT: Fermi Award winners were invited to a DOE-sponsored meeting in Washington in 2005. This is the group, mostly recent winners, that responded to the invitation.

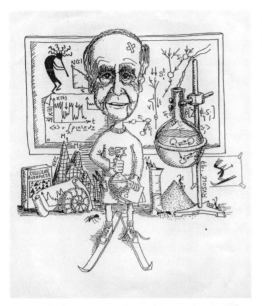

LEFT: One day this cartoon of me appeared on my desk. I never identified the cartoonist.

LEFT: During his term of office as vice-president, Al Gore visited SFI. I had met him as a senator in Washington and briefed him on the activities of the Institute. He was deeply interested and eventually responded to my invitation to visit us.

BELOW LEFT: Senator Jeff Bingaman became the senior senator from New Mexico when Pete Domenici retired. He has also expressed his interest in the work of the Institute. This picture was taken at a gathering of the Bingaman Circle, an organization of major Bingaman supporters.

37 The Santa Fe Institute: Its Intellectual Origins

The Aspen Institute discussions reawakened my interest in finding common ground between the relatively simple world of natural science and the daily, messy world of human affairs. I felt that more participation by natural scientists would make it possible to explore the nonlinear dynamics of social systems. If the gap described by Snow were to be closed, it seemed that the initiative had to be taken by natural scientists. It was physics that had made a mistaken virtue of avoiding "soft" science. The Senior Fellows at Los Alamos shared my views. We soon invited several Visiting Senior Fellows to join our discussions. One of them, David Pines, was a prominent member of the National Academy who seemed to know everybody and was a constant source of helpful suggestions. Another was Nobel Laureate Murray Gell-Mann.

By early 1984 we agreed to create an educational institute that would operate in Santa Fe. Nick Metropolis and I visited with Jack Campbell, former governor of New Mexico, to enlist his help in incorporating our new enterprise. He immediately agreed to draw up the necessary papers. We proposed a name, the Santa Fe Institute, but it belonged to an existing organization that treated alcoholics and drug addicts. We incorporated in May 1984 as the Rio Grande Institute. When the earlier Santa Fe Institute became defunct months later, we changed our official name to the Santa Fe Institute of Science.

We began to discuss the nature of the new campus in more detail. Predictably, the participants proposed a wide variety of possibilities.

Would it be an undergraduate college, a graduate university, or a research center? Herb Anderson, noting our differences, said, "Let's invite some of the very best people we know to a meeting in Santa Fe and ask them what topics are of greatest interest to them." Murray Gell-Mann said that he had been hoping for years to develop a campus that would have no departments and that would move into intellectual territory at the interfaces between the conventional disciplines. We agreed to sponsor a meeting on the theme of "Emerging Syntheses in Science." Gell-Mann's prestige helped us attract the attention of eminent scientists who were already fully committed elsewhere.

In the beginning, the group paid little attention to finding money. Murray muttered that there must be a rich widow somewhere who would give us three hundred million dollars. I had hoped that David Packard, a fellow member of the WHSC and founder of Hewlett-Packard, would become a sponsor. We discussed a possible agenda. David said he had been raised in Colorado and loved the New Mexico area. However, back at Stanford he made a very large donation to extend the campus in order to pursue programs similar to those we had discussed in Washington.

I was encouraged by enthusiastic support from my old friend Arthur Spiegel, son of the founder of the Spiegel Catalogue Company. Art had left Chicago as a young man and moved to Albuquerque to become an investment manager for a number of institutions and southwestern Indian tribes. He gave us the use of his office staff and telephone and attracted initial donations from a number of local corporations. He used his contacts in Chicago to obtain an appointment with a principal in the administration of the MacArthur Foundation. The Foundation pledged twenty-five thousand dollars. Meanwhile, Murray visited the Carnegie Foundation in New York and received an additional twenty-five thousand dollars.

Our proposed workshops were now funded. They were held at the School for American Research in Santa Fe on October 5 and 6 and November 10 and 11, 1984. The participants were selected to represent a wide variety of interests in the natural and social sciences and mathematics. I chaired the meeting. Murray led off with a far-ranging survey of the emerging syntheses in science, from particle physics and cosmology to what he called highly complicated systems, starting with the life sciences. Connections between different fields became even more evident in the many talks that followed. We struggled to find a term that would embrace their commonalities and settled on "Complexity." Later our mantra became "Complex Adaptive Systems" (CAS).

Warren Weaver published a seminal paper in 1948 in *Science* that discussed science and complexity. Two-body problems, the main focus of classical physics, are described as simple. The general behavior of millions of reasonably identical bodies, each acting unpredictably, can be calculated with the aid of probability theory and statistical mechanics. These he called the problems of disorganized complexity. He then turned his attention to systems involving numbers of particles, agents, or bodies, more than two or three but much less than millions. Systems of this kind are encountered in biological, medical, psychological, economic, social, and political sciences. They behave in an organized way. He called these the problems of organized complexity and noted that, although they are well described, the underlying processes are poorly understood. Weaver then asserted that, within the next fifty years, science must learn to deal with the problems of organized complexity.

I can't recall that anyone at our first meetings referred to Warren Weaver's paper, but it must have had an important impact. I was attracted to the theme because, despite their diversity, scientists attending the meeting defined the word "complexity" in ways that embraced their various interests. The word provided a broad canopy. There are many kinds of complexity and many definitions. In the most general dynamical terms, systems are complex when the differential equations that define their states at any given moment in time cannot be analytically solved. Simulated behaviors can be described by models that involve numerical computations, usually on computers, but precise predictions are not possible. Existing models don't simulate emergence, a term that means the whole is more than the sum of its parts.

38 SFI Becomes Operational

At organizing meetings we appointed a board and elected Murray Gell-Mann as chairman. I accepted the job of president. It involved continuing the effort to provide the money necessary to make the new institution a reality. Murray continued to talk about needing three "units." His unit was one hundred million dollars.

I visited Eric Bloch, head of the National Science Foundation, and asked for support. His reaction was favorable, but he noted that all of the NSF funds were allocated to conventional disciplines. I said that we would immediately become a conventional research institute if we sought funding for individual research initiatives from the various divisions. Bloch understood the problem but had no category at that time for highly interdisciplinary efforts. His deputy suggested taxing each of the divisions in order to provide $250,000 a year in support of the Institute. He agreed. Highly encouraged, I then visited with Al Trivelpiece, Director of Research at AEC, described the Institute, and told him of the offer of help from NSF. Al had the same problem as NSF in broadly funding an interdisciplinary center. He decided to use the NSF formula of taxing each of his disciplinary divisions in order to allocate an additional $250,000 a year in support of SFI.

It took nearly two years to formalize these funding arrangements, hire staff, find quarters, and plan our first research programs. Throughout all of our discussions of initial focus, I remained particularly interested in the new field of molecular biology. It was being pursued in various institutions by experimental biologists, biochemists, biophysicists, and theoretical physicists and had become a poster child for fruitful interdisciplinary research. I assumed that our first efforts would probably build on these remarkable advances. There was no lack of challenging topics. Our newly formed science advisory board quickly endorsed efforts by George Bell and Alan Perelson to organize a workshop on theoretical immunology. They were leading researchers at Los Alamos in this new field. The workshop convened in June 1987. Probably everyone who had become interested in theoretical immunology was there. They were a small number. A major topic was modeling the dynamics of various aspects of the immune response, a complex, adaptive system. The immune response refers to the body's ability to recognize and destroy potentially harmful invaders. It dealt with an increasingly urgent problem. The HIV epidemic, the spread of a virus that attacked the immune system, could no longer be ignored. The Institute gave the workshop a high priority. It was the first of its kind.

As president of SFI, I had to make decisions, sometimes controversial, about the breadth of our interests. Murray invariably referred to our mission as inclusive of all of science from elementary particle physics and the beginnings of the universe to founding a large degree-granting university. Our discussions became more detailed.

We all agreed that the center would have no departments. However, we scaled the university concept back a couple of orders of magnitude. We would not establish a degree-granting graduate school. There was universal agreement that we would not be a think tank that provided legislative options to policy makers. The think tank might come later with a separate building and staff. We would establish a modest research center, home to a small number of eminent scholars who combined depth of knowledge with broad interests. They would appoint a number of post-doctoral students. We would have a skeleton supporting staff. We would invite outside scientists to spend sabbaticals or extended visits at the Institute. I visited the Salk Institute and Rockefeller University to get their by-laws as models for our own. Josh Lederberg, head of Rockefeller, advised me strongly to limit our research to problems that involved controlled laboratory experiments.

Lederberg's advice was sound but proved to be too constraining for our purposes. I particularly wanted SFI to help close the gap between the worlds of natural science and the social sciences. We couldn't do everything, and I favored novel dynamical treatments to additional emphasis on phenomenological descriptions. Murray continued to describe a much broader agenda that encompassed "simplicity and complexity." We were all reductionists at heart and wanted to believe that nature was inherently simple. But, in practice, I did not insist on connecting complex systems with simplicity. We couldn't pick our way through emergence. There were no unique paths back to the simplest origins. We agreed with Murray when he referred to historical accidents at times when nature had options and seemed to toss a coin.

At the outset, our interest in the life sciences dominated our activities. In July 1987 Harold Morowitz, a professor of biophysics at Yale, led a summer school for graduate students on "The Matrix of Biological Knowledge." It was quickly followed in September by a workshop led by Stanford's Marc Feldman on computational approaches to evolutionary biology. In the same month we sponsored, together with Los Alamos, another first, a conference on "Artificial Life" led by a creative young maverick, Chris Langton. It was our most popular meeting and had to be moved to the city auditorium to accommodate about 125 attendees.

I was approached by Stuart Kaufman, a professor at the University of Pennsylvania and a consultant at Los Alamos. He wanted to join the SFI staff. His credentials were outstanding. He was both a physician and a theoretical physicist. I seconded his appointment. His interest was in the origin of life. He was taking a different approach, the notion of an autocatalytic chain that closed on itself and self-replicated, compared to the theme Harold Morowitz was pursuing, the complex series of reactions producing long carbon-based molecules that would eventually reach a replicating protein-like configuration. I felt that the Morowitz/Kaufman interests represented the potentially most important theme at SFI and gave them my full support.

The chain of events that would explain how a self-replicating protein was first made is at the heart of the controversy between creationists and evolutionists. Evolution is not the central theme of the argument even though creationists focus on it. Intelligent design says that the Designer made the first self-replicating life form, moving in one step from long-chain carbon molecules to the protein to the cell to the organelle to the organ and to the organism in the form of the first man. They allow that modifications in a given organism can occur by Darwinian selection, meaning that less successful life forms get killed off. But evolution makes no effort to account for the invention of self-replication in a protein. A plausible biochemical explanation of self-replication at this level of complexity should force intelligent designers to challenge science at that point rather than at the level of Darwinian evolution that assumes the existence of living things. How did those first protocells begin to replicate?

September 1987 saw the Institute agenda expand beyond biology and into economics. The motivation was not simply intellectual. It was a topic of interest to one of the nation's leading bankers who offered to fund an economics program at SFI. It all started when Bob Adams, a member of our board and head of the Smithsonian Museum in Washington, discussed SFI with John Reed, then head of Citicorp. Bob suggested that John come to Santa Fe with a few of his staff to talk about some of the problems in international finance that his company was attempting to solve. I arranged a meeting, cochaired with Bob Adams, at Rancho Encantado, a charming resort just outside Santa Fe. We discussed various initiatives in economics and related social sciences. At the end of the meeting Reed offered to fund a long-range program at SFI on the global economy.

Our September meeting on "Evolutionary Paths in the Global Economy" was organized by David Pines and was cochaired by Phil Anderson and Ken Arrow, Nobel Laureates in physics and economics respectively. The meeting began with a review by Professor Arrow of his major contribution to social science, a highly mathematical, physics-like approach to neoclassical economics. It led to the Arrow-Debreu concept of general equilibrium, a concept they termed intertemporal equilibrium. The physicists had a different view of equilibrium and felt that economics was too complex for the elegant Arrow-Debreu approach. After several days of spirited discussion, it was agreed that SFI would undertake a program that challenged the assumptions of perfectly informed and perfectly rational agents, two necessary conditions for the Arrow-Debreu model.

In a conversation with me following the meeting, Professor Arrow indicated that he was pleased by the decision and wished to continue his involvement with SFI. When he returned to Stanford, he persuaded his fellow faculty member, Brian Arthur, to join the resident faculty at SFI and direct the new program. Arthur joined the staff in mid-1988 and led the program for the next fifteen months. Arthur introduced some unconventional ideas that received wide attention and now appear to be conventional. Among these was the notion that many modern innovations require a very large front-end investment in order to achieve acceptance and success in the marketplace. This line of argument suggested that the government should be the lead investor in highly advanced computer technology. It had a significant impact on government policy.

39 Behavioral Science

By 1991 I felt that SFI was well established and that I could turn the presidency over to someone who might bring in fresh ideas. I then chose to pursue an interest in psychology and neuroscience, subjects in which I was a complete amateur. I felt that advances in neuroscience, largely based on new brain-imaging technology, might provide deeper understandings of patterns of human behavior, the province of psychologists.

Many of my questions arose from my decades-long association with the Manhattan Project and postwar Los Alamos. At the end of World War II I became involved, along with many other veterans of the Project, in discussions about the control of atomic energy. We believed that the atomic bomb had played a decisive role in ending the war with Japan. But it was immediately apparent that for major nations war was no longer a rational option. The invention and demonstration in 1952 of an enormously more devastating thermonuclear bomb simply reinforced this conclusion. However, there always remained the possibility that irrational governments or, sooner or later, groups of terrorists might gain access to these weapons and use them.

I was concerned that cultures that tolerated and even nurtured violence could lead to a catastrophic nuclear confrontation. The manipulation of the German people by Hitler shook my faith in the rationality of society. Perhaps even more disturbing, in the 1940s and 1950s and even now in a somewhat different context, there have been advocates of a U.S. "preventive" war. When, if ever, would a preventive war in a nuclear age be justifiable?

I hoped that we could avoid a nuclear war for at least a generation. The problem would then pass to those yet unborn. So I began to pursue the notion that lasting behavioral patterns are formed in the very young. If we learn how to provide appropriate early environments to all children, a significant proportion of them might be more critical and successful than my generation has been in finding pathways to sustainable peace and global well-being.

These interests have led me to explore a fascinating and complex topic, identification of critical factors that help shape behavior and development in individuals, particularly during the first three to five years of life. I decided to use my own early childhood and subsequent development as a fragmentary but informative case study. I hope that the reminiscences I have included here suggest how some of the interactions with my environment have shaped my adult interests and behavior. If so, they may have some general value.

Babies are born with intense curiosity and powers of observation. A fascinating book on early development is called *Scientists in the Crib*, by Gopnik, Meltzoff, and Kuhl. It stresses a baby's drive to examine anything new, to categorize and remember, to imitate. Very early in life babies can be ranked in mental skill by the time they spend with novel experiences. The highest-ranking babies quickly lose interest in repetitive exposures to the same thing. They seem to be saying, "I've been there and I've done that. What's new?"

Curiosity tends to diminish with age as the brain learns and remembers how to respond to an enormous number of experiences with the use of "scripts." Children who retain their vigorous and critical curiosity into adulthood remain scientists in spirit, regardless of what professions they pursue. They examine carefully and look beyond easy answers. Although learning by rote may earn good grades, it doesn't foster the kind of curiosity that makes for good science.

Let us consider some of the underlying factors that generate patterns of individual and social behavior. There are commonalities in the sensory inputs and responses of cells, organisms, and aggregates of organisms. A major part of research at SFI is concerned with the nature of communication and response between members of a community of organisms, for example, microbes, ants, bees, or primates.

Cells communicate with one another and with their surrounding environments largely through chemistry. The chemistry channels of smell and taste are important in insect communities but vision, touch, and sound also contribute. Humans use all their sensory channels. They are unique in the extent of use of spoken language to communicate with other members of their society. They pass beliefs and behavioral patterns, both examined and unexamined, from generation to generation through culture.

Modern technology is telling us a great deal about the critical importance and details of early development. In a baby inputs from all sensory channels are used to connect an exuberant growth of dendritic fibers into neuronal circuits that categorize and respond to all aspects of daily life. If the environment provides too few stimuli as, for example, for most of the babies in an average orphanage, cognitive, social, and emotional skills do not develop normally and behavior may be pathologic. There is a considerable body of data supporting the notion that children raised in enriched environments tend to have superior mental skills.

At present in the United States most parents have jobs outside the home. For many babies much of the day is spent in an environment that fails to adequately promote their potential mental skills. We mandate that all children go to school at age five or six but are much less concerned with their development during their earliest years of life. Their performance when they reach school suffers in comparison to children in many other societies. Most prosperous countries make professional care for infants and toddlers available to all families. Evidence is growing that these long-term investments, designed to increase the proportion of vigorous, inquiring minds, ultimately pay rich dividends.

When children grow up, their early histories greatly affect the way in which they participate in their societies. Their work skills determine where and how they earn a living. They form various groups that aggregate into hierarchies of organizations and institutions. These different clusters are nodes in connected networks that interact and help define the nature of the world in which they live. If we hope to see all nations move toward desirable and mutually sustainable goals, we must insure that these increasingly important groups, many of them nongovernmental organizations, are fully informed, innovative, and connected.

40 My Interest in Early Mental Development

We now see a growing recognition of the importance of early development, but there are considerable differences of opinion about the nature of inputs that contribute most effectively to mental skills. I felt that it was essential to get more specific real time information concerning the connections between early environment and development. This kind of information could best be obtained through collaborations of researchers in neuroscience and psychology. In developmental psychology the major measures of the effect of early inputs have been eventual outcomes. Measurement in real time of the effectiveness of various environmental inputs would be greatly strengthened by demonstration of their relationships to the early histories of regional neuronal activity and eventual outcomes.

I began my studies in neuroscience with a trip to the University of Chicago where I sought advice from Professor Jack Cowan. I read several books that he recommended on neurophysiology and neurochemistry. I was puzzled by the fact that development of behavior and development of neural activity were two separate fields of research that seemed only remotely connected to one another. I contacted Dr. Bela Julesz at Rutgers University, a physicist who had turned to neuroscience. I asked him to help me organize an interdisciplinary workshop at SFI on the plasticity of the brain. He became chair and principal organizer of a workshop we held in Santa Fe in 1993 on "Maturational Windows and Adult Cortical Plasticity." It brought some of the leading researchers in neuroscience and psychology to SFI. Many of them became visiting scientists to the institute and helped organize a follow-on workshop in 1995. It was on "Intervening to Enhance Child Development" and was chaired by Dorothy and Jerome Singer, psychology professors at Yale.

In early 1996 Ellen Goldberg, a biologist and dean at the University of New Mexico, became president of SFI. She quickly showed a deep interest in early development and helped bring together a group of psychologists and neuroscientists from Rutgers University, McGill University, Harvard University, the University of Washington, and UCLA. We organized a workshop to explore relationships between the development of behavior in infants and toddlers and development of patterns of localized activity in the brain's cortex. This is the part of the brain that receives, processes, and responds to incoming information from the senses. These functions depend on the existence of many billions of neurons in the cortex. Neurons are cells that communicate with each other through enormous numbers of connected circuits. The circuits transmit electrochemical pulses through junctions between neurons called synapses.

A neuron contains a fat portion called a soma that houses the cell nucleus. The soma forms a cord-like extension called the axon that signals other neurons downstream in a neuronal circuit. The soma also forms many other extensions called dendrites that receive signals from neurons upstream in the circuit. When an incoming signal from dendrites produces a sudden change in a voltage gradient across the cell membrane, the resting potential of the cell is transformed to an action potential or "spike." It propagates along the axon to a little button that interfaces with a target cell at the synaptic junction. The button produces a burst of particular kinds of molecules called neurotransmitters that move to the target cell. The target cell then continues the message transmission to other neurons by triggering another action potential at the target cell's soma.

A single neuron is connected directly to ten other neurons and indirectly through neuronal chains to thousands of other neurons. In sharp contrast, a computer "neuron" is connected to only two neighbors. This difference helps account for the fact that brains have computing power comparable to the largest electronic computers despite the fact that incoming messages are processed about one million times more slowly. Because their structures and mode of operation are entirely different, brains are able to perform functions that modern digital computers simply can't undertake.

The human brain is about 2 percent of total body weight but demands about 20 percent of the body's energy. Most of this energy is spent maintaining the resting potential of neurons and restoring it following action potentials. Energy is provided by blood flowing through a network of arteries and capillaries to the vicinity of every active neuron. Physicians and researchers use blood flow to watch the brain at work. They do this with a now familiar technique called magnetic resonance imaging, MRI for short. The energy required to restore the resting potential of a neuron after an action potential is provided by a spurt of oxygenated blood to the neuron. It metabolizes glucose and becomes deoxygenated hemoglobin. The MRI machine is able to read the ratios of oxygenated to deoxygenated hemoglobin as a function of time and region in the brain. This information is used to produce well-resolved images of brain structure in space. They can produce single images at a moment in time. This function is called structural MRI (sMRI). When many images are strung together over a longer period of time, they make a movie of the ongoing neuronal activity. The movie-making process is termed functional MRI (fMRI).

The brain constantly performs many functions that are more or less automatic and subconscious. These activities produce underlying levels of signals in the fMRI process that are called the resting baselines. It is not yet possible to sort out the nature of the various individual events that contribute to resting baselines. An incoming sensation from the external environment is processed by neurons that attend to the activated sensory channel. If the incoming signal is provided by an experimental neuroscientist, the neuronal activity produces a little peak about 1 percent higher than the underlying baseline. The additional signal is called an evoked response. When various sensations are provided to the brain by the investigator, the regions that record them are identified and a detailed functional map of the brain can be constructed. If a patient shows symptoms of brain disease, the map can help identify the nature of the problem.

Babies are born with a lot of programmed neuronal circuits that enable them to perform the tasks necessary for immediate survival.

However, the brain is born prematurely. In order to develop normally it must form many new circuits. Instructions from the external environment augment those received earlier from genes.

A normal baby will look, hear, feel, smell, and taste with an urgency and an ability to categorize and remember that will never be duplicated in later years. The brain produces enormous numbers of fresh dendrites, some of which are programmed into a vast new library of behavioral patterns. If the external environment fails to provide a high level of stimulation of the various senses, the new dendrites are not programmed and, consequently, not provided with nourishing blood. Unused dendrites wither and disappear. Babies raised in sterile environments, in poorly attended orphanages, for example, are likely to suffer from serious developmental pathologies.

The science that describes the formation of patterns of behavior in infants and toddlers is called developmental psychology. Although neural development of the brain must underlie all externally observable behavior, little is known about early details of postnatal, regional wiring of circuits and effect of differences in environment. Babies aren't subject to neurological measurements unless they have significant medical problems. Most of what is known about early brain development is based on animal research.

Jeff Hawkins, inventor of the PalmPilot, has written a remarkable book entitled *On Intelligence* which suggests the way the cortex, the thin outer envelope of the brain, computes and governs our behavior. His proposed design has almost no resemblance to electronic computers. He asserts that the major functions of the cortex are to remember previous experience and to predict the future, moment by moment. These functions shape our behavior. He was motivated to write the book, in part, by a desire to persuade an upcoming generation of computer scientists to design hardware and write software that can operate in patterns similar to those that are used by the cortex. He believes that such machines, departing radically from current computer designs, are inevitable. I think that the book is a good read for those who like to speculate about how brains really work.

The group we assembled at SFI to consider relationships between developmental psychology and neuroscience included some outstanding researchers in these fields together with pediatricians, biologists, and chemists. They examined progress in MRI technology and agreed to its intensive use in an innovative program to examine the way the neural structure and activity of a new brain develop over the first three years of life. I hypothesized that such studies would demonstrate relationships between behavioral patterns studied by developmental psychologists and regional development of neural circuits in the brain studied by neuroscientists.

Neurons in the baby's brain quickly sprout many new dendrites that become active, shape behavior, and require additional blood flow to supply their demand for energy. Cerebral blood flow increases by as much as a factor of five in the first three to four years of life as these neural patterns are formed. If the environment is not sufficiently stimulating, as for example in a crowded orphanage, fewer patterns are formed and most of the new dendrites atrophy and disappear. The process is commonly called "pruning" and occurs to some extent in every developing brain. We assume that mental skills improve in children raised in appropriately stimulating environments and have attempted to explore how patterns of behavior are related to details in the regional demand for blood.

Now named the Santa Fe Institute Consortium (SFIC), group members recruited hundreds of infants to participate in repeated fMRI examinations and other measures of regional neural development. A major problem had to be solved. About ten minutes of run time are required for each fMRI study. During this period the subjects must be motionless which requires that they must be sleeping. Sedation isn't permitted. As a result, the investment in time and money is high. For the first three years, financial support of SFIC activities was provided by the Institute. The program continues at the various campuses with locally available resources. Results are beginning to appear in papers published by the participating teams. In coming years the results should help provide detailed insights into the way various regions of the brain program neural circuits during the early years of life.

Research on early mental development is a growing field in psychology and neuroscience centers. It is increasingly evident that many children are raised in environments that penalize their cognitive, social, and emotional skills. Conventional wisdom tells us that a loving caretaker, usually mother, provides all that is needed in a child's early years. But a large majority of today's mothers are at work during the day. Substitute nurturing environments, such as those provided by trained babysitters or competent day care centers, are expensive and frequently unavailable.

In the United States we recognize a social responsibility for nurturing children when they reach kindergarten age. However, we assume relatively little responsibility in earlier years. Most other prosperous countries, in both eastern and western parts of the world, pay much more attention to their youngest citizens. But there are signs of change in this country. Numerous efforts are being undertaken at social and political levels to include the earliest years of life in our concern for the young. It requires a considerable increase in school and childcare budgets, but once the startup costs are paid, the social and economic payoffs will surely more than repay the bill.

Programs like those initiated at SFI will make instrumentation available that can routinely measure levels of regional neural activity in a benign and noninvasive way and provide early warning of the occurrence of any of a number of developmental pathologies. Of equal or greater importance, if information is also gathered about the child's external environment, including details about day care, our ability to provide appropriately nurturing care, tailored to individual needs, will be much improved.

41 What Have I Learned?

I believe that the most important single factor that shaped my career was my early environment. There were also random turns. If the record were played again, the outcome, for better or worse, would be different. Good luck was vital. But something in the way I was reared made a crucial difference. My curiosity wasn't turned off. I always felt rewarded when I learned something new.

Curiosity is essential but not sufficient. It must be accompanied by a capacity for critical thinking. Unlike curiosity, the critical faculty is not innate. It must be learned and constantly practiced. We are encouraged to accept authority and to believe what we are told. Learning by rote in school is necessary, but it doesn't encourage wrinkled brows. Standard curricula should offer courses in how to think critically. I suspect that there is a major shortage of people who can teach these skills. In a rapidly changing, increasingly complex world, the need to encourage critical thinking is becoming desperately urgent.

But an imaginative mind also needs to escape formal constraints. Language is an art form. The imagery of poetry adds an essential dimension to communication. My high school English class was instructed by a true lover of literature, Alice Shaughnessy. She wanted to know what books I read and suggested that some of them were not worth the time. She offered substitutes, Thomas Hardy for P. G. Wodehouse, for example. She followed my progress, talked with me after class, and put me on the board of the high school literary magazine where she continued to monitor my work. I owe her a great debt.

When I became seriously engaged with science, I added still another dimension to my world of communication. Good physical science relies heavily on mathematical expressions. But I never resonated to the formal rules of mathematics in the same way that I did to imaginative literature. We pay a price for an increase in rigor. Imagination can transcend formalities.

I improved my social skills more slowly and imperfectly. My part-time involvement with banking has provided numbers of opportunities to interact with business and community leaders. But the people I particularly seek out are usually in the academic world. Many of them are provocative and more self-regarding than average. I suspect that I share these qualities. The person who has had the greatest success in polishing my manners is my wife, who gently corrects my gaffes and still smiles at me each morning at the breakfast table after more than sixty years of marriage.

As the years have gone by, I have observed a connection between lively curiosity and good health. The people I knew who made a virtue of their existing expertise and, in effect, retired early appeared to be less vigorous than those who remained curious.

My wife and I were both exposed in our professional careers to much more radiation than the average person. We are struck with the contrast between our longevity and popular beliefs about the supposedly deadly nature of our earlier work environments. It's not just that we are fairly healthy and outliving the predictions of the actuarial tables but so are many of our associates. Several have died but not from their exposure to radiation. Almost all my lost friends had fatal heart attacks, not a disease associated with low-level radiation. Not a single occupationally irradiated colleague of mine at Los Alamos has died of leukemia or any other type of cancer, problems frequently attributed to low-level radiation. A few were victims of accidental exposure to massive doses of radiation. Louis Slotin and Harry Daglian killed themselves at Los Alamos in the 1940s pursuing their jobs in ways that would now be considered incredibly reckless but were common then when getting the job done quickly took priority over safety.

Strangely, the elevated exposures most of us have experienced over the years may have been beneficial rather than harmful. This is not the official view of the various health boards that set permissible levels of exposure. Their ruling is that risk is linearly proportional to exposure level and that this conservative assumption will change only if carefully controlled longitudinal experiments clearly demonstrate that it is wrong. Such experiments will be so difficult to organize, expensive, and prolonged that they will probably never be undertaken.

I believe in a nonlinear response to cell damage by radiation. Cells constantly renew themselves and repair low-level damage. I can find no evidence that the repair mechanisms distinguish particular sources of damage. Although there is no doubt about the harmful effects of large amounts of radiation, the assumed increase in cancers and other possible pathologies among a population exposed to low-level radiation is so small compared to the incidence from other causes that existing data are essentially irrelevant. It is extremely difficult to estimate the level of exposure of any individual to low levels of radiation. Unreliable anecdotes underlie most estimates of possible damage from chronic low-level exposure.

Increasing life expectancy can have both positive and negative consequences. It's generally true that more old people are remaining relatively healthy. Our skeletal structures become weaker but can now be partly replaced with artificial joints. As neurons are inevitably lost and cell connections become more fragile, our mental skills decrease. Alzheimer's disease and other geriatric brain pathologies are becoming more common. The personal and economic costs are high. The overall social costs are more difficult to estimate but constitute a major problem. Hopefully, they will be mitigated in coming years by advances in neuroscience.

42 What Lies Ahead?

For the first time in history, we have the power to destroy much of modern society and return to primitive times. It is imperative that natural science and social science, working together, become more effective partners in achieving deeper understandings of human behavior, the constructive use of the many forms of power, and the avoidance of major wars and terrorist catastrophes.

It is clear that behavior is governed by the brain. Many research tools are expanding our knowledge of neuroscience and early mental development. The use of imaging and functional probes like fMRI (functional magnetic imaging), EEG (electroencephalography), MEG (magnetoencephalography), and PET (positron emission tomography) tells us a great deal about where the brain processes sensory inputs and activates the visible and vocal responses that constitute behavior. Its operations are programmed by countless neuronal circuits, some of them wired by genetic instructions from genes in the womb and others by signals from the environment following birth.

Yet, despite our remarkable progress in neuroscience and developmental psychology, we have only the most rudimentary understanding of how the brain encodes and uses its enormous library of information. We are increasingly aware of the importance of emotions but have only a fragmentary understanding of the neurochemistry that orchestrates them. Our vast ignorance provides fascinating opportunities for discoveries in neuroscience and, quite possibly, for radically different approaches to computer design and programming. Even very limited success can redefine our notions about neural and mental processes. Our goals should not be modest. For an upcoming generation of young students, I can think of nothing more rewarding than addressing the question, "How does the brain really work and govern behavior?" The times have never been more favorable.

Currently, a researcher who uses fMRI as a tool will probably examine only responses to carefully selected signals, like touching a right thumb or reciting a rhyme. The instrument then measures an increase in the regional neural activation of a particular part or parts of the brain. The increase will be about one percent over the activity that is already there, the so-called baseline. There is little or no information concerning what functions are represented by this baseline activity despite the fact that it presumably is the major part of what that region of the brain is doing. Emotional responses probably get triggered in the baseline. It would open a valuable new field of research to identify the various baseline tasks that occupy so much of the time and unconscious attention of the brain.

43 Power and Complexity

Power has a simple definition in physics. Its meanings are more various and quite different when applied to human affairs. The definition I prefer is the ability of an individual to shape the behavior of others. It can be expressed as the fraction of the group of addressed individuals that behaves in the way desired by the seeker of power. Throughout life my own behavior has been shaped by the pursuit of power or its exercise by others. My work on the Manhattan Project involved coercive power. In a more benign way, it has taken the form of intellectual argument. Economic and political forces have always been important. The theme of power is particularly relevant to aspects of SFI research that focus on complex human behavior.

Power is central to all the creation myths. External Beings imposed order on chaos or created it from nothing. Human society could not have survived without nurturing order imposed by power. It's a timeless topic. Machiavelli wrote a treatise on power, *The Prince*, five centuries ago. Countless books continue to be written on power. Among the modern efforts, I have particularly liked John Kenneth Galbraith's brief *Anatomy of Power* and Adolph Berle's more searching treatise on *Power*. They have helped me enlarge my understanding of the forms of power.

My lifelong tendency to question authority has been affected by my involvement with the sciences of complexity. It has provided me with a somewhat different understanding of the ubiquity of power in human affairs. The innate behavior of individuals can be highly complex. Although the rules within various societies around the world vary widely, they must all deal with complexity and, as a result, share common patterns. Almost invariably, they construct social and economic hierarchies of authority and power coupled with spiritual hierarchies. Their cultures contain many constraints, often coercive. Religious mandates came first, enforced by powerful witch doctors and clerics. The Ten Commandments established the primacy of monotheism. Hammurabi's Code came later. Engraved on stone, it spelled out a commonly practiced Babylonian system of civil and religious law that punished a wide variety of crimes with death. European civil law, developed and codified in recent centuries, has helped humanize the uses of law in Western society and has increasingly served as a basis in secular societies to nurture order. The Constitution of the United States established the first government in which a judicial branch shared power with and potentially dominated the legislative and executive branches.

If any society chooses to leave most potential degrees of freedom unconstrained, the inevitable result is chaos. When a power vacuum exists in society, an individual or small group seizes control and enforces order. All stable societies are highly constrained. Morality may be necessary in the long run but, in the past, stability has often been achieved for substantial periods without it. A colleague at SFI, Sam Bowles, argues that altruism informs power and conveys survival advantages. It has become an important innate and cultural force that develops over millennia through a kind of Darwinian social selection.

Historically, the most practical function of culture, including religion, has been to prescribe and constrain behavior. The power to enforce these restrictions is usually placed in the hands of relatively small numbers of people. To survive over centuries, leaders of societies have had to provide for contributions by innovators and nonconformists. Completely authoritarian governments, including theocracies, have little tolerance for innovation and become vulnerable.

A revolutionary new threat has emerged in recent decades. It represents a potential phase change in human affairs. Smaller and smaller numbers of dissidents can obtain the means to destroy the physical fabric of societies. Governments are searching for ways to mitigate this threat. The contributions of scientists will become increasingly important.

In 1948, before this threat began to loom large, Warren Weaver wrote a paper on "Science and Complexity" that speculated on the role of science in human affairs. I think it is appropriate to quote his closing words:

> If science deals with quantitative problems of a purely logical character, if science has no recognition of or concern for value or purpose, how can modern scientific man achieve a balanced good life, in which logic is the companion of beauty, and efficiency is the partner of virtue?
>
> In one sense the answer is very simple: our morals must catch up with our machinery. To state the necessity, however, is not to achieve it. The great gap, which lies so forebodingly between our power and our capacity to use power wisely, can only be bridged by a vast combination of efforts. Knowledge of individual and group behavior must be improved. Communication must be improved between peoples of different languages and cultures, as well as between all the varied interests that use the same language, but often with such dangerously differing connotations. A revolutionary advance must be made in our understanding of economic and political factors. Willingness to sacrifice selfish short-term interests, either personal or national, in order to bring about long-term improvement for all must be developed.
>
> None of these advances can be achieved unless men understand what science really is. All progress must be accomplished in a world in which modern science is an inescapable, ever-expanding influence.

Weaver was prophetic. His advice has become urgent. I fervently hope that we will use our exploding knowledge of science and technology to better teach us how the brain and mind work and govern our behavior. We must learn how to raise children who, as adults, are able to deal with complexity more skillfully than we have to date. The price we may pay if we fail can be, for the first time in history, the survival of a coherent society. Cormac McCarthy, a Santa Fe Institute faculty member, has written *The Road*, a very dark picture of the evil that our new power to destroy may bring to the world. We must help the next generation ensure that his frightening vision is not prophetic.

Index

Kurchatov, Igor, 93
Kwajalein Island, 54–55, 65, 95, *95*,
    96, *96*
Kyger, Jack, 33

Laboratory Senior Fellow, 116
Lande, Irv, 46, 52
Langham, Wright, 53, 55
Langton, Chris, 147
language, 159; arbitrariness of, 6
Lawrence, Arthur, 133, *133*
Lawrence, E. O., 26, 133, *133*
Lazarus, Roger, 82
Lederberg, Josh, 146
Levin, Bob, 133, *133*
Libby, Bill, 68–69
Lindberg's solo flight, 10
Livermore lab, 63; Los Alamos v., 75
Los Alamos: alcohol at, 52–53; for
    Atomic Energy Commission, 55;
    banking at, 78–81; conference
    at, 84; debris samples to, 65;
    disposition of, 78; driving at,
    48, *48*; financial institutions at,
    78–79; as home, 71–73, 83; housing
    at, 71–72, 78, 80–81; Livermore
    lab v., 75; private ownership of,
    78–79; radiochemistry at, 42–43;
    recreation in, 82–83; return to, 59;
    Santa Fe and, 72–73; secrecy and,
    52, 59; TA-1 at, 49, *49*; Truman to,
    61; utilities at, 79; Western Area in,
    50, *50*
Los Alamos Building and Loan
    Association, 80–81
Lucky Dragon 5, 68–69

MacArthur, Douglas, 16
Machiavelli, 164
MAD. *See* mutual assured destruction
magnetic resonance imaging (MRI), 155
Mallinckrodt Company, 33
Manhattan, 42
Manhattan Project, 1–2, 150; hazards

from, 34; power and, 164; prologue
    to, 29–32; Russia and, 93
Mark, Carson, 75, 82–83, 98, *98*
marriage, 47, *47*, 51, *51*, 55
Masius, Morton, 1, 24, 25
mass 235, mass 239 v., 26
McCarthy, Cormac, 166
McCune, Marshall (Marr), 72–73
McCune, Perrine, 72
McMurdo Station, 117–21
MDA. *See* Mutual Defense Agreement
Meitner, Lise, 1
Meltzoff, 151
Meltzoff, Andrew, 3
memoir, purpose of, 2
Memoirs (Teller), 82
memory, 3–4, 8, 14, 130
Metal Hydrides, 30
Metallurgical Laboratory. *See* Met Lab
methane, 118; mass 21 and, 116–17
Met Lab, 33–37, 48, *48*
Metropolis, Nick, 82–83, 142
Mike: duplicating, 88; fission and,
    66; neutrons in, 66–67; radioactive
    debris from, 65–67; Russia and, 74;
    testing of, 64–65; as thermonuclear
    device, 62–65
military, 77; exemptions from, 39–40,
    46, *46*
molecular biology, 145–46
Morgan, Frank, 89–90
Morgan, Janet, 90
Morowitz, Harold, 147
movies, 11–12
MRI. *See* magnetic resonance imaging
Murrow, Edward R., 76
music, 6, 14, 21, 57; opera, 20, 73
mutual assured destruction (MAD),
    127
Mutual Defense Agreement (MDA),
    89–90

NASA, 124
National Security Agency (NSA), 75

Turkevich, Anthony (Tony), 64

Ulam, Stan, 62, 69–70, 74, 82–83, 98, *98*
United Kingdom: atom bomb development in, 27; collaboration with, 89–90; gas fraud from, 126–27
University of Chicago, 1, 153. *See also* Met Lab
university years: academics in, 22–24, 46, *46*; employment in, 22–23; essay award in, 23; lab discovery in, 22; reporting in, 23; uranium fission story in, 1, 24
Upton, Arthur C., 133, *133*
uranium: from Creutz, 31; deposits of, 108; isotopes, 26–27, 106; natural, chain reaction with, 29; neutrons and, 66; at Oklo, 106–8; production plant for, 33; sources of, 30–31; temperature and, 30
uranium-235: in nuclear weapons testing, 42–43; plutonium-239 v., 29; theft of, 86; uranium-238 v., 26–27
uranium-238: neptunium-239 and, 26; plutonium-239 v., 29; uranium-235 v., 26–27
uranium-239, plutonium-239 v., 29
uranium atom: atom bomb v., 1, 26–27; chain reaction and, 1, 24; fission story and, 1, 24
uranium metal: diamond saws for, 35; hazards of, 30–31, 35–36; production of, 35; sources of, 30–31

uranyl nitrate, 29–30
Urey, Harold, 26
USS *Estes*, 64–65
USS *Nevada*, 96

vaudeville, 11–12

Wahl, Art, 91
war: atomic bomb and, 27, 150–51; petroleum and, 23
Warner, John (Jake), 52, 55
Washington, 75, 117. *See also* White House Science Council
Watkins, James D., 140, *140*
The Way of All Flesh, 11–12
Weaver, Warren, 144, 166
Weisskopf, Victor, 127–28
Western Area, 50, *50*
Westinghouse, 31
White House Science Council (WHSC), 116, 123–24
WHSC. See White House Science Council
Wigner, Eugene, 25–26
Wolfsberg, Kurt, 114
Women's Suffrage Amendment, 5
Worcester, Massachusetts, 9
Worcester Polytechnic Institute, 1, 47
Wu, Madame C. S., 42

X-rays, 34–35

York, Herb, 63, 75

Zia Company, 72